JAPAN TODAY!

A Westerner's Guide to the People, Language and Culture of Japan

THEODORE F. WELCH, Ph.D.   HIROKI KATO, Ph.D.

PASSPORT BOOKS
NTC/Contemporary Publishing Group

ABOUT THE AUTHORS

Theodore F. Welch is former director of the Center for the Study of U.S. Japan Relations at Northwestern University and has resided in Japan for over 13 years since 1954. Fluent in Japanese, he has received training in Japanese at the undergraduate and graduate levels, including a Ph.D. from the University of Tokyo. With a wide range of experience in private and government sectors, Dr. Welch brings not only linguistic competence, but knowledge of Japan in his own professional area of information science. He is currently professor of Japanese at Northern Illinois University, DeKalb.

Hiroki Kato is vice president for Asian Development at the Chicago Mercantile Exchange, and until 1989, was Associate Professor of Japanese at Northwestern University. With a Ph.D. from the University of Chicago, he taught sociolinguistics at the University of Hawaii, and has taught at Harvard. Bilingual in Japanese and English, Dr. Kato has been an observer of the role of language in the two societies. Beyond language, he looks at behavior, institutions, and business as well as other customs which form the patterns of Japanese character. He has long been an interpreter of American manners and mores to his fellow Japanese.

This edition first published by Passport Books,
a division of NTC Publishing Group.
4255 West Touhy Avenue,
Lincolnwood (Chicago), Illinois 60646-1975 U.S.A.
First edition published under title *Japan Connections*.
Copyright © 1990, 1986 by NTC Publishing Group.
All rights reserved. No part of this book may be reproduced,
stored in a retrieval system, or transmitted in any form
or by any means, electronic, mechanical, photocopying,
recording or otherwise, without the prior written
permission of NTC Publishing Group.
Manufactured in the United States of America.
Library of Congress Catalog Card Number: 89-63655

8 9 ML 9 8 7 6

INTRODUCTION

Handy yet comprehensive, *Japan Today!* is an indispensable guide for anyone seeking basic information about Japan. Business people, veteran and first-time travelers, educators, and students will find this book invaluable for gaining real insight into the Japanese people, their language, and culture.

The wide range of topics in *Japan Today!* includes facts about the country and how it is run, explanations of Japanese terms and customs, and a variety of subjects of a cross-cultural nature. Arranged alphabetically, they can be located quickly and easily. The Table of Contents functions as a complete index to the subjects covered in the book. In addition, a system of cross-references (identified by "*q.v.*") allows the reader to find out more about other items related to the same topic.

Because *Japan Today!* offers many comparisons between the U.S.—or Europe—and Japan (for example, on education, the economy, housing, customs, and culture), it will be a great aid to those doing business and dealing professionally with the Japanese. At the same time, it provides useful information on travel, accommodations, and use of free time. There are also detailed explanations of cultural concepts, uniquely Japanese, that are essential for anyone who wants to relate effectively to the Japanese.

Also included, at the back of the book, are a section on the language (covering pronunciation, common Japanese names, basic expressions and vocabulary, and numbers), a selected bibliography, and an appendix with valuable information for traveling in Japan.

Whatever your travel or professional needs, *Japan Today!* will be your key to understanding Japan and the Japanese.

TABLE OF CONTENTS

viii

JAPAN TODAY!

A

Abacus

It is hard to imagine that the abacus *(soroban)* is still a popular mathematical device in the land of the modern electronic calculator. Historically, the major instrument for teaching arithmetic, the abacus is still very much in use, and appears in a variety of shapes, sizes, and colors. Basically a handheld set of moveable beadlike counters placed parallel to each other on rods, the *soroban* is a tool with sturdy roots in the business and educational traditions of the Orient. It was introduced into Japan from China in the 14th Century. The flicking of the beads within the abacus frame provide a strong tactile and visual impression when it is used regularly. Great speed and facility have been developed by most Japanese, to the point where contests have shown the abacus to be as fast as electronic devices. A "mental" *soroban* has enabled many to make calculations in their heads. It is not uncommon to see Japanese figuring numbers with an imaginary abacus, their fingers moving in air while they visualize the positions of the beads. Although generally displaced by its electronic cousin, the abacus is kept under the counter by many shopkeepers as a back-up for really tough mathematical assignments.

Acupuncture

The basis of acupuncture *(hari)* is the placement of needles, from one to three inches in length, deeply into the human body at various locations. Done properly, the process is painless and, in fact, relieves pain, often immediately. The target of the puncture is a nerve or muscle impairing the proper function of internal organs. This treatment, introduced from China in the 6th Century, involves the strategic placing of very thin needles made of gold, silver, or platinum into more than 600 possible locations of the body. The needles are pushed or hammered into selected areas to relieve physical or mental ailments. The needles draw no blood. The methods vary according to the school of practice, and acupuncturists are licensed by the government. The treatment can be habit forming, and some addicts require daily sessions owing to reliance upon the instant relief received. No medicines are used in acupuncture.

Administrative Guidance

Administrative guidance, or *gyosei shido*, is a practice employed by government in Japan to exercise influence over the private sector.

Although business enterprise in Japan is regulated by domestic and international laws and agreements which are binding, administrative guidance, which is in fact powerful government pressure, is not founded in law. It is a bureaucratic custom that has its roots in feudalistic authority. Japanese enterprises have long lived with, and expect, government "guidance." Foreign businesses are no less subject to this workable but non-legal system of government interference. In practice, the various agencies employ persuasion in what is a typical Japanese approach to decision making, in this case, what is best for the country. Although bureaucratic guidance is an indirect means of coercing private enterprise, Japanese companies appear to prefer it to more overt means of regulation. From such large-scale measures as controlling the flow of money, to more minor but irritating tactics of administrative red-tape snares, the government's power is well known. Non-Japanese find it impossible to operate a large-scale business enterprise in Japan without the assistance of knowledgeable and influential men, who themselves may well have been employees of such giant agencies as the Ministry of International Trade and Industry (MITI, q.v.), the Ministry of Finance, or the Foreign Office. Administrative guidance is a two-way process wherein the government's programs are achieved in concert with a wise and willing private enterprise sector. The industrialist is under no obligation to comply with bureaucratic suggestions, but he realizes that it is part of the social and economic fabric of his country.

Affection

See Also: AMAE; DATING AND MARRIAGE

Public display of certain emotions is avoided in Japan. Affection for one's spouse or friend of the opposite sex is not exhibited. Although young people today can be seen holding hands, rarely is a kiss exchanged in public. Hugging is a rarity. This is not to suggest that the emotions of love and affection do not exist, but rather, they have their proper place indoors and out of sight of others. This reflects the deep sense of propriety and discretion embraced by the Japanese. Non-Japanese are wise to refrain from showing affection for Japanese friends when greeting them. Kissing on the lips, the cheek, hugging, arms around the shoulder, etc. are actions very unsettling to Japanese.

Ainu

The aborigines of Japan who once inhabited much of the land but were pushed to the northern tip of Honshu in the 8th Century and ended up in Hokkaido and the islands further north. In terms of social history, the Ainu can be likened to the American Indians. From earliest of times they have sustained hardships and struggles with the dominant peoples who now form the main composition of the Japanese society. They maintain a specially protected status by the government, and because many have married into the mainstream, their numbers have dwindled to less than twenty thousand. Ainu men have deep black hair, splendid mustaches and beards, and are tall of stature; women tattoo their faces above and below the lips. The Ainus are among the hairiest races in the world, having come from Siberia. Traditional Ainu dress, which can be seen by visiting their settlements near Sapporo, favors gay and fancy design. Ainu villages are tourist attractions for Japanese and foreigners alike.

Airlines

See Also: AIRPORTS; TRANSPORTATION

A sizeable list of international carriers provide service to and from Japan, and there are also a number of domestic airlines. Tokyo telephone numbers are provided in the appendix.

As a service to hotel guests, international flight updates, cancellations, delays, and other changes are shown on television and announced in English over Channel JCTV wherever this cable TV service is available.

Airports

See Also: AIRLINES; TRANSPORTATION

The two major international airports are at Narita (Tokyo International) and Itami (Osaka International).International departures occur from other airports, most notably Haneda, located between Tokyo and Yokohama. Narita is the major airport and is located northeast of Tokyo in Chiba Prefecture. By auto or airport limousine bus the trip into central Tokyo can be less than an hour under ideal conditions, and nearly two hours when the limited access highway is congested. The airport is new, and offers excellent facilities, including convenient stopover hotels nearby. Transfers to connecting flights, foreign and domestic, are expedited with typical Japanese efficiency. In addition to auto/airport-limo traffic into Tokyo, trains are available via the Keisei Line, or by Toei subway. In any event, reaching the final destination in Tokyo is likely to entail several transfers (unless a very expensive taxi ride from door to door is preferred). A direct airport-to-hotel bus service operates to major Tokyo area hotels, with return service available. The Tokyo City Air Terminal (TCAT) is one point of arrival for the airport bus, and on the return trip can serve as the check-in counter for most airlines. From the TCAT, located in the Hakozaki area of Tokyo, a taxi to the hotel is reasonable and convenient, although a bus to Tokyo Station leaves frequently. From the Tokyo Station a variety of transportation is available to all parts of Tokyo and Japan. In addition to the above modes of commuting between Narita and Tokyo, there are other rail and bus services available, but they can be complicated when language is an obstacle.

Osaka International Airport is the gateway to southwest Japan (the Kansai area) and is convenient when direct travel to Osaka, Kobe, and Kyoto are required. Bus service to and from Osaka station is 25 minutes; to and from Kobe, 55 minutes; and service is approximately an hour to or from Kyoto. Airport limousine service between major Kansai hotels is dependable and inexpensive.

Haneda International Airport, which serves mainly as a domestic airport now, is within a half-hour ride from central Tokyo by monorail, which is pleasant and reliable, especially during rush hours. Direct baggage transfer service between airports is provided by Air Baggage Service Co. Porter service is also available. A schedule of representative costs can be found in the appendix.

All-Girl Revue

Foremost among the musical revues that have flourished in modern Japan is the Takarazuka group, which gets its name from a pleasure resort located between Osaka and Kobe. The troupe also performs in Tokyo in its own resident theater near the Ginza (*q.v.*). The women play all of the roles in the musical renditions of Japanese and foreign stories. Specialists in men's, children's, and elderly roles have a popular following nationwide among women of all ages, who idolize their favorite stars. In contrast with Kabuki (*q.v.*), which is an all-male cast performing serious drama, the Takarazuka resembles light opera in the West. Other entertainment involving all-girl dances, songs, and comedy are found mainly in nightclubs and restaurants. They range from the expensive *Cordon Bleu* (with its topless dancers) to the *Shichi-Go-San*, where kimono-clad folk dancers welcome volunteers to join in from the audience.

Alphabet

See Also: ROMANIZATION

Strictly speaking, the Japanese language is not written in an alphabet, but rather in Chinese characters, *Kanji*, and phonetic symbols, *Kana*. However, the alphabet as English speakers know it is used when romanizing the sounds of the Japanese language. Also, the alphabet is used in a variety of ways and places and the Japanese are familiar with it. Foreigners are advised to learn the Japanese pronunciation of the alphabet as an aid in spelling foreign words, such as when spelling their own names orally. The "equivalents" are as follows:

a = ay as in bay	j = jay	s = esoo
b = bee	k = kay	t = chee/tea
c = she	l = ehroo/ehdoo	u = you
d = dee	m = ehmoo	v = voo-ee
e = ee	n = ehnoo	w = daburu-you
f = efoo	o = oh	x = ekksu
g = jee	p = pea	y = wye
h = ay-chee	q = cue	z = zetto
i = eye	r = ahroo/ahdoo	

Amae

Perhaps the most important psychological concept used to explain many Japanese behavior patterns, *amae* has been variously translated as "dependence," "indulgence," and the like. The most fundamental *amae* is found in the love and attachment an infant feels towards its mother, who is unfailingly caring and dependable. In return for such absolute love, the infant learns to reciprocate with devotion and obedience. A typical Japanese person seeks *amae* in almost any person-to-person relationship, such as in the student-to-teacher relationship, a subordinate-to-superior relationship in an organization, or even within a temporary relationship between a passenger and a flight attendant. In essence, *amae* represents a desire to place total trust and confidence within a hierarchical human relationship. The psychology expressed by *amae* is not unknown in the West; but in Western cultures, maturing has meant acquiring personal autonomy and independence, thus repressing the need for *amae*. Some "child-like" behavior of grown Japanese men and women is a not-so-subtle expression of the *amae* psychology.

Architecture

One of the first impressions of a foreign land is the difference in the culture evident by its architecture. Japan incorporates a variety of styles, much of which in the larger cities is "Western" at first appearance. Indeed, skyscrapers have taken on a universal character. And yet, as one looks closely, even in the metropolitan areas like Tokyo and Osaka, there are motifs of oriental architectural detail on modern buildings, on small shops, and on homes. The further away from the city centers one travels in Japan, the more distinctively Japanese the homes and other structures appear. From the beginning, when temples (Buddhist) and shrines (Shinto) were constructed, the contrast between continental Asian and indigenous styles were apparent. Proponents of architectural theory hold that the simple, unpainted wooden structures devoid of ornamentation are the natural side of Shintoism inherent in Japanese nature. Shrines, the outdoor and indoor styles of farmhouses, and unfinished concrete are said to be part of this affinity with natural things. Temples, with their colors, detail, carvings, and intensity of ideas elaborately carried out are but still another manifestation of the acceptance the Japanese have for opposites. Styles are allowed to exist side by side, even blended, without giving offense to the selective eye of the Japanese viewer. Visitors to Japan will seek out what is "purely" Japanese, and come away wondering just what it is they have been seeking.

Japanese homes have *tatami* floors, which are made of straw mat. The shoes are removed in the *genkan*, which is a street-level entrance in the front of the house. One goes up into the home (hence, "*o-agarikudasai*," "please come in" — literally, "come up"). Separating the *tatami* are *shoji*, or sliding doors with paper covering. Guests are seated in front of the *tokonoma* (alcove), which is the center of attention in the main room, and which serves many purposes. While the guest is there, a table may be present, around which all will sit on *zabuton*, or pillows. Dinner may be brought into the room and served at the table. In the winter, a heavy cloth would be placed over the table to keep in the warmth of the *kotatsu*. Japanese homes are rarely centrally heated or air conditioned. After dinner, that table is removed and a *futon* spread out for use as the bed. The flexibility of the Japanese house allows for multiple uses of most of the rooms.

Asakusa

This popular amusement district, located in the eastern section of Tokyo, is one of the oldest and best known pleasure centers of Japan. Modern movie houses, theaters, restaurants, temples, and a host of other attractions bring the Tokyoite, the out-of-towner, and the foreigner all seeking excitement. On New Year's Day the famous Asakusa Kannon Temple draws a crowd so large as to defy a head count. The serious and frivolous exist side by side. Foreigners enjoy walking the side streets, for their quaintness suggests to the knowledgeable that these were the licensed gay quarters (i.e., brothels) of ancient tradition that still continues, only less obviously. Asakusa can be reached by train or subway during the day and evening, and by taxi or chartered bus (sponsored by tour groups) late at night. Because of the many small bars and clubs there, Asakusa at night offers a fascinating glimpse of local color, but the first-time visitor should be escorted by a knowledgeable local host. As a favorite location for the working class, Asakusa is the poor man's Akasaka, another section of Tokyo known by foreigners for its shops and entertainment spots. A number of discos and foreign food restaurants are located in Akasaka, not far from the Hotel New Otani, the Akasaka Prince, the Ana Hotel, and the Hilton.

Atami

A "warm sea" (hence, *Ata-mi*) resort one hour's fast train ride from Tokyo. One of the most popular and flourishing hot springs centers in the country, it has many of the traditional *ryokan* Japanese inns. Situated close to Mount Fuji, it is favored for its view of Japan's favorite mountain as seen from the coastal splendors of the Izu Peninsula. Atami is believed to be part of an extinct volcano, which would account for the abundance of hot water bubbling up from countless sources in the area. Nearby, Hakone, Izu Skyline Parkway, Mt. Fuji and the island of Oshima draw visitors from all over the country on weekends, especially in the summer.

B

Baby Sitters

For those requiring this service, the hospitality desks of major hotels maintain lists of available Japanese adult women who are willing to sit with children. The Tokyo Domestic Service (see appendix) provides a list of qualified sitters. If one is needed and hotel or business service is not available, a number of possible sources are listed in ads in the English-language newspapers. Volunteer service groups, with ads in newspapers, telephone books (English editions are available in hotels and tourist agencies), and on church bulletin boards are good sources to check out. Live-in students are a possibility for the new resident.

Ballet and Modern Dance

Development of Western-style dancing, particularly ballet, has lagged behind the advancement of symphonic musical performance and the opera in Japan. However, announcements which appear regularly in the newspapers attest to the ballet's ascendancy. Longer and sturdier legs on the smallish Japanese body have resulted from the post war dietary changes, and these have in turn lifted the ballet from a second class citizen in the art world to a viable competitor for the attention of the music and theater buff. Many excellent dancers can be seen in performance of the Momoko Tani Ballet Company and other modern dance ensembles.

Banzai

A well-known shout, or hurrah, which means "ten thousand years." It is used to cry out or chant enthusiastically about a person or celebrity, such as the Emperor, with respect to his long life and good fortune. Although it is associated with the battle cry of the Japanese military, it predates historical Japan, and comes from China, its earliest usage dating back to several centuries B.C. A foreigner is most likely to encounter the usage today when witnessing a crowd of well-wishers at the airport, or at a train platform; perhaps the promotion of a colleague or the parting of a company executive on an important assignment is the context. It is often shouted in threes, with arms raised together above the head, as though the participants were signaling a winning touchdown at an American football game.

Barber Shops

The major hotels in the larger cities are accustomed to cutting non-Japanese hair, and have sufficient English skills to get the job done to one's liking. The basic price of a haircut and shampoo under these circumstances is considerably higher than a similar service in a barber shop in the suburbs, or in the countryside. It is worth the experience, and considerably cheaper (including a head and neck massage) to visit the shops which Japanese frequent.

Bars

See Also: ENTERTAINMENT

Aside from the cocktail lounges in the dozens of foreign style hotels in Tokyo and other major cities, it is difficult for the non-Japanese to find an atmosphere that he or she can relate to. There are many private clubs to which non-Japanese may belong, but these are either costly or inconvenient to join. In a country literally loaded with watering holes, the general rule is to go drinking with someone who knows, or is, a Japanese. Japanese frequent several favorite haunts, where they are always known and where a tab is kept. No money changes hands when a Japanese goes drinking. The drinking spots are tailored to the social status and economic prowess of the clientele, and so walking into an unknown bar is a strange experience, especially for the management and the local frequenters. A superficial effort may be made to accommodate a foreign stranger but the systems employed are not geared for the casual or sudden encounter. Sticking to the hotels and advertised spots (consult the newspapers and the tourist guides in the hotels) where the foreigner is not only expected but welcomed is the best procedure until an invitation to a genuine Japanese bar is forthcoming.

Inside a typical bar is seating enough to accommodate about a dozen or two. Invariably a "mama-san," who runs the place, will drop by and spend a few minutes with her regulars, getting acquainted also with their guests. In many of the bars (actually small clubs), hostesses nearly equal the number of guests, and their function is to provide lively and titillating contact, including jokes, innuendos, light parlor talk and songs. A growing phenomenon is the *kara-oke* bar. Here, the guests and the hostesses sing along with prerecorded (sometimes live piano) music, minus the melody, which is to be supplied on the spot. Mikes are passed around and the talented and tone-deaf alike join in, much to the delight of others. It is not unusual for a Japanese host to take his foreign guest to several of these spots in one evening.

Baseball

Introduced from the United States in 1873, baseball has become the most popular sport in Japan. High school and college contests attract crowds which are equal to or even larger than football crowds in the United States. Professional baseball is the king of all professional sports; the first pro-ball team, the Yomiuri Giants, was established in 1934. Today there are a dozen teams in two leagues, the Central and Pacific. The winner of the "Japan Series" frequently plays host to the American World Series winner. Japan is pushing for a true World Series that would determine a winner in an international baseball competition.

Baths

It is well known that Japanese use the bath for both cleansing and relaxation. The communal bath was created both out of necessity (it was expensive to have a bath in one's home), and for the social outlets provided. This was true until after the Second World War. At the community baths, which are still prominent throughout the country but which have become segregated by sex, a large common pool of water serves as the source for washing and relaxing. Because the water is changed once daily, it is important that bathers are clean before they enter the pool. This is done by body washing at individual stations adjacent to the hot pool. These habits extend to the home and hotel; one is clean before entering the bathtub.

In addition to bath houses used by the general public, there are specialty bath houses offering a variety of services. Combination sauna/bath/massage parlors are generally respectable enterprises. These facilities are also available in most hotels.

Beauty Parlors

All major hotels have beauty shops and cosmetic supplies. The English is good and instructions easily followed. In addition to the hotel-based service, there are a number of shops located near the foreign residences and diplomatic enclaves. They include the Azabu district: Maroze (above the supermarket); Roppongi: Sweden Center House of Beauty, and Hollywood; Omotesando: Carita; and Ginza: Yamano. In addition to imported beauty preparations, locally produced cosmetics by such companies as Shiseido are excellent.

Bonsai

Miniature trees placed in shallow trays have for centuries fascinated Orientals, particularly the Chinese and Japanese. Known in Japan as *bonsai* (literally, tray plant), these mini trees and plants have an exotic history as extensive and varied as the forms, sizes and types in which they come. The idea central to this form of domestic art is the encapsulation of natural beauty, a poetic reminiscence of landscape through dwarfing. Today, people everywhere have come to know and admire the well-proportioned specimens of *bonsai* art even if they cannot thoroughly appreciate the great time, skill and care involved in the stunting process.

11

Bonsai were first discovered growing wild. Trees were dwarfed naturally by the elements in locations high in the mountains or along windswept cliffs. As they were introduced into homes, gardens and shrines, they grew in importance and influence, but not in size. Japanese landscaping, often representing distant mountain scenes, fostered the art of selective rockery and influenced the evolution of *bonsai*. Pine, bamboo and plum blossoms — staple decorations at Japanese festivals throughout the year — are perennial *bonsai* favorites. Present efforts to continue to reflect the traditional and timeless genius so closely associated with the true art of growing and training *bonsai* is still the way of the Oriental master today.

Bookstores

Books are published in Japan at a rate equal to that of the United States, and book stores per capita far outnumber those in America. Located in hotels, stations, terminals, shopping arcades, and department stores, book stores carry a good selection of magazines and special interest publications. However, only a few carry books of interest to a foreign visitor. Books written in English about Japan can be found in the hotel book shops. A more comprehensive selection of books in English can be found in several large stores on the Ginza: Maruzen Company (Nihonbashi) and Kinokuniya Shoten, both of which are nationwide chains, and the Jena Bookstore (Ginza 4-Chome).

Bowing

Bowing, one of the oldest of established Japanese customs, is used in greeting one another and saying goodbye. While it is important for the foreign visitor to observe this custom, it should not be overused, as there is a strict protocol to follow when bowing. The depth of the bow and how long one holds it depend on the relative status of the people bowing. Many Japanese, especially the young, expect foreigners to shake hands rather than bow, and follow this practice themselves when greeting them.

Budo

The term means military or martial arts, and embraces most of the self-defense arts popular in Japan, such as judo, karate, kendo, and aikido. Behind the physical and mental development of the individual participant lie the precepts of chivalry as adhered to by the samurai. A closer look at each follows:

Aikido

All of these martial arts sports are undertaken with the assistance of a master, who is a high-ranking and certified instructor. While the other sports have more or less set rules according to the school of instruction and practice, Aikido has no set rules. The student must learn thousands of techniques. But he is first faced with understanding the "matching of spirits" that is the essence of aikido: how the moods and mental strengths of the "opponents" approach each other. This also is part of the "gentle way" of judo.

Judo

This training is aimed at the unarmed person who seeks to discipline and protect himself. Hence, judo means "the gentle way," and was formerly known as *jujutsu*. Although a fighting art originally, it has long become associated with the mental, moral, and spiritual influence it has on the mind as well as the body. Heavy jackets of cotton are worn by contestants in a judo match. A belt and baggy trousers are part of the outfit. A match consists of winning one point, gained when one of the opponents is thrown onto the mat, pinned down for 30 seconds (or until he yields), lifted shoulder high, or is otherwise prevented from continuing. This is accomplished by one or more techniques, such as arm locks, holds, and throws. The judo hall where the great matches are held in Tokyo is the Kodokan.

Karate

Along with the term *jujutsu*, karate is associated with swift and deadly action. Literally "the open hand," it is a school of the martial/self-protection approach which aims at attacking vital spots on the opponent's body. Beyond the use of the hands, kicks, elbowing, and head-bumping are employed to develop a variety of strengths. Thick boards, bricks, etc. are practiced with, thereby increasing one's strength. Karate demonstrations prove the overwhelming ability to split boards, break bricks, and topple objects of great density and weight. All the while, the concentration and sincerity demanded of the practitioner is constantly stressed, so that the sport never loses its relationship to the development of the individual and the serious attitude and spiritual growth it affords.

Kendo

Since the 8th Century the art of swordsmanship has been held in high esteem by the warrior class; with the rise of the samurai class in the 12th Century kendo was held in highest esteem among all the martial arts (referred to as *tachikaki* and, later, *kenjutsu*). Fostered by the All Japan Kendo Federation, the modern version closely follows tradition. In a match, the winner is the one who gets two out of three points, a point being made when a clear hit to the head, throat, trunk or waist is accomplished. A thrust must be accompanied by a shout which names the part of the body being targeted. Appropriate padding, including thigh and shin guards and a shield for the head, is worn.

Bullet Train

See Also: TRAINS; TRANSPORTATION

Racing at speeds of up to 240 kilometers per hour (145 miles/hour plus), the name in English is more descriptive than its Japanese original: *Shinkansen* — literally, the new trunk line. There are two basic train services, according to speed and number of stops: the *hikari* ("light") and the *kodama* ("echo"). The *hikari*, faster because it makes less stops, requires six hours and forty minutes to travel 730 miles between Tokyo and Hakata in northern Kyushu. It makes six stops in between, at: Nagoya, Kyoto, Shin-Osaka, Okayama, Hiroshima, and Kokura. The cost for the trip is listed in the appendix. Sleepers are not available on the *hikari* or the *kodama*, but are provided on the other Japanese National Railways train services. Shinkansen service is also available to cities north of Tokyo — to Niigata and, along the east coast of the country, Morioka. Frequency of trains and the reliability of the timetable make this service a real money maker for JNR. Four trains per hour leave Tokyo station from as early as 6:00 A.M. Bullet Train service is designed to reach the destination before midnight. Both types of trains have a reserved seating system; tickets for reserved seats can be purchased one month in advance. Tickets are available at the Tokyo station or at any of the *hikari* or *kodama* stops along the line.

Bunraku

The puppet drama (*Bunraku*) of Japan is unique in the world of doll theater. The dolls are hand held and manipulated by up to three men each. The men are dressed in black with hoods over their heads, so as not to detract from the dolls themselves. Only the master manipulator's face is seen. Set to the ballad musical narratives of the *Joruri*, the lifelike reality of these dolls stems from the artistic creation of the dolls, the two major schools of interpretation, the music performers who sing and play on the three-stringed *shamisen*, and traditions dating from the 16th Century. The accepted *Joruri* form is the Gidayu-Bushi, developed by Takemoto Gidayu in the late 17th Century. The Takemoto and Toyotake interpretation schools are the surviving dominant schools of *Bunraku*. The head, body, arms, and legs of the dolls, when combined with exquisite costuming, are able to provoke great subtleties of emotion and dynamic range of action, including several movements for each finger. The variety of facial expressions faithfully express the spectrum of human emotions from hatred to love. The National Theatre in Tokyo and the specially designed Asahiza in Osaka (the original home of *Bunraku*) mount performances about three months of the year. Performance schedules are printed in English-language newspapers.

Burakumin

See Also: RACIAL MIXTURE; SOCIETY

Class distinctions are an exception in the homogeneous society of Japan, but there is an outcast group which may or may not live in designated settlements or sections of a city. They are called *burakumin*, which means "special hamlet people." Although many of these people now live outside the original settlements, there still are areas in Japan where *burakumin* live isolated from the rest of society.

From feudal times this group was employed to perform tasks which were considered unsavory, such as the slaughtering of animals. Although these people are racially Japanese, they have found it difficult to marry into the Japanese mainstream, and continue to conduct their affairs on the periphery of societal acceptance.

Bushido

The term refers to the way of the *Bushi* or warrior; hence, the feudal-military code of Japanese behavior. *Bushi* is a term from China, and means "samurai." The original meaning of samurai refers to one who serves, or waits upon. Therefore, in the households of the court ministers and other high officials, the samurai were employed to serve their masters.

Business Hours

Business hours in Japan are much as they are in the United States. Saturdays are considered a day of work in Japan, at least from 9:00 to 12:00. Most everything is closed on Sunday, except some department stores and shops. Department stores are open six days a week, and each has a different closing day. (Hours are 10:00 to 6:00.) Banks are open on weekdays from 9:00 to 3:00, 9:00 to 12:00 on Saturdays. Business hours for major companies and professional offices are 9:00 to 5:00 on weekdays, and occasionally half days on Saturday. Shops and smaller stores are open from 10:00 to 8:00 every day, including Sunday.

Business In Japan
See Also: ECONOMY

The Japanese are devoted to the work ethic. They have come to enjoy one of the highest standards of living in the world. They realize that, in a resource-poor environment, they must deal with the rest of the world in economic terms: buying raw materials and selling goods. Most of the countries they deal with are in different time zones. This means working long if not odd hours to be on the job when telephone or other direct contact is required with business colleagues in other countries. As the free world's second largest economy, the survival instinct has catapulted the tiny island nation into a superpower of the world economic order. "Economic animals" is a rubric they deny, but recognize how it has come into being. From the government on down, Japan is united in its instincts to maintain the well-being of its people now and in the future. "Japan Inc." is the result of this cooperative approach which extends across the entire fabric of society. Yet, the pejorative tone notwithstanding, the concept carries with it a total commitment of all sectors to maintaining the standards of living they have come to enjoy. The arts, sciences, humanistic studies, sports, recreation, travel — all depend upon the economic and business environment that is the first concern of all Japanese.

C

Calligraphy

See Also: LANGUAGE

The writing of Japanese by hand is of concern to both the social and business world of Japan, and its role is firmly rooted in a tradition that has not been allowed to die out. The care with which writing has always been undertaken by the Chinese and Japanese has lifted it to a level of high art. Personal philosophy, morals, and even daily concerns have long been associated with the calligraphic tradition. The very representation of thoughts, ideas, and emotions on paper with ink has been, in itself, a reflection of the state of mind and intentions of the Japanese as they seek to communicate in a medium they have long preferred: the written word. The style of writing, even the shape of the strokes, is an indication of the attitude of the writer. The task of writing Chinese characters, which form the body of the Japanese orthography, far exceeds the skill required to recognize and read them. Because of this, artistic schools of calligraphy have developed. As an end in itself, calligraphy is designed to help obliterate all outside distractions so that the innate meaning of words and phrases can be fully appreciated. Some of this sensibility has carried over into the work-a-day world of modern Japan, with its focus on business.

Foreign businessmen should be sensitive to the role of the written word, not only as it may be typed or otherwise electronically produced, but how the handwritten message is honored in Japan. When foreigners find it necessary, and desirable, to communicate in Japanese, the choice of words and style of writing becomes an essential ingredient. When other means have failed to reach a Japanese individual, a letter written in Japanese has proven to be effective. Care must be shown not to offend the recipient, however, who may be alarmed that his English is seen to be unskilled. Clearly, there are times when typewritten communications are efficient and effective, while on the other hand, the calligraphic approach is not to be overlooked.

Calligraphy is useful also as an ornament, like pictures or flower arrangements. A philosophy is presented, as well as art. Expert calligraphists are highly regarded in Japan, and characters written by them are sought after, and naturally, correspondence received from them is highly prized. Exhibitions of works of calligraphy are frequently held in Japan. It is undeniable that this aspect of Japanese customs reaches deeply into the depths of artistic taste Japanese so much value in life.

Cars And Driving

Domestic and foreign automobiles crowd the landscape of Japan. Although the country is ill-suited to the auto, the love affair goes beyond the well-known ability of Japan to build a better vehicle. Since the 1964 Olympics, a network of limited access highways has connected cities along the eastern seaboard, and intra-city highways are causing at once ease of access to cross-town points and eyesores. Most of the new roads are elevated in the cities, and their stilt-like appearances have removed much of the charm of certain sections of Tokyo and Osaka.

Driving is on the left side and the metric system is in effect. International symbols aid the foreign driver, but many of the signs designating exits are in Japanese. Generally speaking, driving is a frenetic business in Japan, bumper to bumper on most roads much of the time. The cars exist nonetheless, and owning one is a status symbol. They are well cared for, and parking places are limited, especially at home. Japanese drivers are careful and mindful of the other driver, although it may not seem so to the first-time observer. They are willing to come in very close proximity to other cars and stationary objects, and do it with aplomb. Whether in a taxi, a company car, or a private auto, you can be sure that the cost of owning and operating are so high that the property is used with greater care than it would appear.

Cherry Blossoms

Sakura — the national flower of Japan. Unlike the fruit bearing trees of the same name in other countries, the Japanese flowering cherry is unique to Japan. It waits for 51 weeks for its short life of glory, but it is just this juxtaposition of exquisiteness and impermanence that have been so poetically embraced by the Japanese. Unless otherwise stipulated, the word *hana* — flower — means cherry blossom, and the traditional pastime of *hanami* means cherry viewing. Famous sites for viewing the many varieties of this favorite of all blossoming trees exist from Kyushu to Hokkaido. Indeed, beginning in the middle of March, one could follow the progression of the cherry season from Kyushu until late May in Hokkaido. Kyoto, Nara, and Tokyo offer sites at which the merrymakers gather, who sit under the blossoms, drink sake, sing songs, and find out that "no strangers exist when the flowers are in bloom." Most mountainsides, gardens, and public parks have their *sakura*, and the Ueno setting is one of the best in Tokyo.

Children's Day

Children's Day is celebrated on May 5, and is called *Kodomo-no-hi*. Since ancient times, May 5 was celebrated as the Boys' Festival. But since the war, the day has included girls as well. Girls also had a special day, March 3, which is no longer a national holiday, but is celebrated just the same. On March 3, *Hinamatsuri* is observed by arranging dolls of the Imperial Court in the *tokonoma* (alcove, and place of honor in a Japanese-style room) on a dais covered by a red cloth. The emperor and empress, along with courtiers and courtesans, complete the entourage. Special cakes and other delicacies are served to the girls and guests in the home. On May 5, and for several weeks before and after, flying carp (*koi-nobori*) are displayed in the yard to indicate the number of members in the household. Similar symbols of youth reaching manhood are on display in the house as a reminder that boys become men through hard work, diligence and obedience. Samurai dolls and other military regalia are symbols of the discipline required of adults. In turn, Children's Day is a reminder to adults to cherish and take care of their children.

Chopsticks

Chopsticks, referred to in Japanese as *hashi*, or *ohashi*, are eating utensils. Unlike the Chinese originals from which they are derived, Japanese chopsticks are neither tubular nor square-ended. Generally they are shorter and conical in shape, but they come in all sizes, shapes, and colors, and have usage beyond their role as a tool for eating. Metal chopsticks are used for putting charcoal on braziers, and oversize chopsticks are used by cooks for stirring and picking up food. Chopsticks should never be used to pass an item to another set of chopsticks, as this is reserved for passing cremated bones at funerals. Also associated with the dead are chopsticks which are stuck into rice and allowed to remain upright. In Japan, Japanese food is invariably eaten with chopsticks, while Western utensils are provided for non-Japanese food. When taking food from a common dish used by more than one person, the non-eating ends of the chopsticks are used.

Christmas

Christmas is celebrated in Japan but it is not a national or, for most people, a spiritual holiday. (Less than two percent of the population is Christian.) The commercial trappings of Christmas are apparent everywhere, and gift exchanging at Christmas time has been incorporated into the Japanese year-end gift-giving custom. The reverence and serenity of Christmas afforded in Western countries is reserved in Japan for New Year's. On the other hand, Christmas is a time for partying and merrymaking, somewhat like New Year's Eve in the United States.

Chugen

See Also: GIFTS AND GIVING

The Chinese concept of dividing the year provides the setting for the widely observed tradition of *Chugen*, namely a period of mid-summer. The usual date for *Chugen* is July 15, and around this day Japanese give midyear gifts. This gift giving is done in the same spirit as the gifts given at year's end. Company bonuses are usually given twice a year, with the *Chugen* being the first. The year-end gift is the second. This custom of giving also coincides with the traditional *Obon*, or All Soul's Festival. At the time of *Chugen*, stores promote special sales to attract *Chugen* purchases. Both individuals and companies send gifts to those in whose debt they are, and to bosses, relatives, friends, and clients.

Climate

Although three of Japan's four main islands lie in the temperate zone, there are significant differences in climate owing to the long latitudinal span of 15°. Okinawa (*q.v.*) and Hokkaido (*q.v.*) are prefectures *(q.v.)* located at both extremes; the former is tropical, receiving no snow, while the latter is under snow as much as five months during the year and enjoys mild summers. The majority of the nation experiences four distinct seasons with time and extent of each varying according to locale. Humidity and rainfall are especially heaviest in the summer, and in the southwest, owing to the influence of the Pacific Ocean. The winters are typically dry, although it snows on the four main islands.

The rainy season (*tsuyu*),brought on by early summer monsoons, occurs for about one month, from mid-June to mid-July. Farmers plant rice just before this period. The typhoons visit in late summer and early fall with their violent storms aimed usually at the southwestern part of the country, although the Kanto area (the district embracing Tokyo and its environs) is not always spared.

The weather in central Japan is often compared with that of New York and Washington, D.C. Summers are damp and hot, winters with clear blue skies. Autumn is pleasant and a consistently favorite time for sightseeing and, in late October, viewing of fall colors. From late March, spring offers the spectacular but short-lived (about a week) cherry blossom season for which Japan is reknowned.

Clothing

In modern Japan, both Western and Japanese clothing is worn. Western clothes are worn to work by both men and women. In the fall, winter and spring, most men wear suits. During the summer months, they leave their jackets at home. On formal occasions, such as marriages, funerals, and visits to the shrine, Japanese women and girls wear kimono. Men and boys do wear formal kimono, but much less frequently.

During the summer, a light version of the kimono, called the *yukata*, is worn around the home and at summer resorts. Western shoes are never worn with kimono or yukata, which require *geta* (*q.v.*) or *zori*. After work, men change into kimono or yukata at home.

Company Structure

The products of Japanese companies compete in the marketplaces of most advanced countries. Yet, the structure and nature of typical Japanese companies reflect many traditional attitudes and values. In some ways, Japanese companies can be likened to "families." Employees tend to regard their superiors as "parents," and superiors are expected to take personal interest in the affairs of their subordinates. Just as a family does not disown a member, except under very special circumstances, a Japanese company does its utmost to retain its employees. Although it is not always possible in small companies, the "life-time employment" system is the society's norm. Wages are paid according to seniority, defined primarily as the length of service with the organization, rather than a reflection of individual ability or achievement. This wage system is called *nenko joretsu-sei* (age seniority system). Companies normally recruit new employees once a year directly from colleges or high schools, and put new recruits through long and rigorous training, which includes lessons in how to speak properly within the organization. The Japanese company is said to hire personality rather than specific skills and knowledge. From the company's viewpoint, its needs may change over a period of time and along with them requirements for specific skills. An employee is expected to be retrained or reassigned to meet new and unpredicted needs of the company.

The retirement age has been long set at 55, but many companies have recently been retaining their employees on an annual basis beyond that age. Loyalty of the Japanese employee to his company is well known; such loyalty is fostered in return for a company's offer of both economic and psychological security. It may appear strange to American business people, but human and personal factors are, at least outwardly, placed above profit considerations in most Japanese companies. Decision-making in the Japanese firm or factory tends to be done collectively, and slowly, often with a new idea arising at the rank-and-file level. Consensus is sought from the bottom up, rather than top-level decisions being imposed upon the rest of the organization. The process of seeking consensus in a company is known as *ringi*, meaning "document circulation." One comparison often made between Japanese and American companies is that Japanese companies tend to be concerned about the wishes and welfare of employees, whereas American business tends to be first and foremost answerable to the stockholders. If an American company does not show profit in four consecutive quarters, it is considered to be in trouble. Some Japanese stockholders are known to wait for four years before they question the productivity of their company.

Credit Cards And Travelers Checks

International credit cards are accepted by Japanese business and entertainment enterprises, with some exceptions. Major department stores prefer cash. But American Express, Visa (affiliated with Sumitomo Bank), Diner's Club, and MasterCard can be used for lodging, meals and shop purchases at major hotels, specialty shops, and some *ryokan* in urban areas. Travelers checks are equally accepted. Passports are often required when cashing travelers checks. Personal checks are not accepted unless drawn on a Japanese bank. Even then, use of checks at point of purchase is rare in Japan, because the Japanese themselves do not use them. There are a number of credit cards exclusive to Japan, and places accepting them show the stickers in the window much as is done elsewhere in the world. While not impossible, it is cumbersome for foreigners who are not long term residents to establish credit card accounts.

Crime

The extremely low crime rate in Japan is due to a number of factors. The makeup of the society, with its conformity to rules, causes extreme care on the part of all not to act in a way offensive to others. Great care is used in preventing crimes, usually committed by members of society not belonging to a neighborhood. Burglaries are guarded against by citizen groups who keep an eye out for strangers on the street. Even in large cities, these groups exist and report to a police station or *koban* (usually a box-like small hutch with room for several officers; identified by the red light above the door).

Another reason for good crime control is the police force itself: large, highly educated (over half have college degrees) and well-equipped with communication aids. While police are armed, they rarely use weapons. In 1980 the number of shots fired in the line of duty nationwide was just one. Hand guns for civilians are strictly forbidden, and most crimes of passion are not fatal. The quiet efficiency of the police is further evident in the riot squads who are disciplined, tough, and trained in the martial arts, including the tea ceremony for restraint and mental discipline. The major crime among the youth of the country is drug usage. Partly due to the extreme pressures on teenagers to succeed in school, and in part related to the ease in trafficking narcotics, the highest crime rate in Japan today is drug abuse by adolescents.

Currency

The currency of Japan is the yen. Denominations of bank notes are: ¥1000, ¥5000, and ¥10,000. Coins come in denominations of ¥1, ¥5, ¥10, ¥50, ¥100, and ¥500. Yen can be purchased at Japanese retail banks in the United States, at the airport before departure, at the airport of arrival in Japan (24 hour service is available at Narita and Osaka), or at major hotels and banks in Japan. Foreign currency is accepted only at a limited number of hotels, shops, and restaurants for direct purchases. Taxis and airport limousines do not accept foreign currencies. A valid passport is required to purchase yen, and the rate of exchange varies little from one place to the next. The variation occurs in the current daily rate of exchange. Gone are the days when $1.00 bought ¥360; the fixed rate for over 25 years following the Pacific War. Since 1971 the rate has fluctuated, hovering around the ¥250/dollar rate. Recently the rate has dropped below ¥150/dollar.

The yen is rising in value at a rapid rate. Daily quotations are posted in authorized places of exchange and in the English language newspapers. Foreign exchange quotations are often quoted in value/dollar. Unused yen can be exchanged back into foreign currency prior to departure, most conveniently at the airport bank. Yen can be removed from Japan up to a limit of ¥5,000,000 ($30,000 or so).

Custom Duties

For the occasional visitor on a tourist visa, custom duties upon entering Japan are virtually non-existent if there is nothing to declare. Duty-free allowances for alcohol and tobacco are: 3 bottles, 400 cigarettes, 100 cigars, 500 grams of other tobacco products, two ounces of perfume, and two timepieces. The latter may be taxable if the value is more than ¥200,000. Prohibited are: firearms, pornography, narcotics. Japan is very strict about these items and punishments are stiff. Those who have shipped items separately must fill out a declaration of unaccompanied goods in order to assure their entry into the country. Upon leaving Japan, tax-free purchases must be declared. This is usually accomplished by showing the passport to a customs official, who will remove purchase records placed there by merchants from whom goods were purchased. Rare art objects and antiques need certification from the seller that they are not national treasures which are not allowed out of the country.

Custom duties for businessmen bringing items into the country are more complicated. It is advisable to check with the local office of the Japan Trade Center (or JETRO—Japan External Trade Organization—in smaller cities) before departure to get updates on recent tariff reductions. Japan, under pressure from the U.S. and Europe in particular, is regularly lowering duty rates and eliminating tax altogether on certain items intended for sale in Japan.

Customs

See Also: CLOTHING; FOOD AND DRINK; DATING AND MARRIAGE; FUNERALS; GIFTS AND GIVING

Many of the social customs not treated specifically elsewhere in this book can be identified as the various subtleties of personal interaction. Outward show of respect for others and their feelings are values taken seriously in Japan. Closely tied to language use and the role of gestures, the social protocols are many and varied. Those customs that foreigners can directly participate in are (1) avoidance of loud and boisterous behavior; (2) speaking in respectful tones, especially to one's elders; (3) using hesitancy as a strength, not a weakness, when speaking, eating, and during other social activity by deferring to others; (4) showing gratitude for any generosity or favors, especially upon the very next time of contact (Letters are not used as much in Japan as the "thank you" note is in America. One is expected to verbally recall the last meeting as having been a pleasant occasion.); (5) Japanese laugh both at humorous stories and when they are embarrassed. These two basically different situations are easily confused by the unknowing foreigner.

It is not difficult for Americans to become familiar with national and local customs, and indeed such familiarity is welcomed as a sign of sincerity and friendship by the Japanese. A quiet and subtle approval will be won by those who care enough to respect Japanese ways and follow these ways with interest.

D

Dating and Marriage

Before the end of the Second World War, marriages in Japan were considered by custom and law as an issue between two households rather than just the union of the two individuals. The head of the household, usually the eldest male, had the final, often all, the say about whom his offsprings should marry. Marriages, for the most part, were the events arranged by the consenting parents with family needs as their primary concern. A go-between *(nakodo)*, who was known to both parties, introduced a candidate pair and served as an intermediary between the two parties. It was not rare that the marrying pair had never seen each other before the wedding. Such strictly arranged marriages have been replaced in the post-war era by new customs where attraction between two people and their own wishes are considered more important in making the marriage decision. Yet, the majority of young men and women still expect to be introduced at first to prospective mates by go-betweens. Dating begins only after the first arranged meeting. It is not uncommon for a young person to be introduced to different people until he or she meets a satisfactory partner; thus, such introductions (called *omiai*) can occur as many as five times or more. There are, of course, couples who find each other on their own. Once dating has begun, either through introduction or on one's own, it proceeds much the same way as in America. Courting may or may not end in marriage. When the couple decides to marry, a go-between couple is sought to play a traditional and purely ceremonial function.

Since dating in the Western sense is a relatively new custom in Japan, young people are found to be much shyer during early face-to-face encounters. Because marriage is seen to be the end result of the period of dating, the Japanese take the matter more seriously from the outset than do Americans.

The marriage ceremony itself may be conducted in a purely Shinto ceremony, or it may have a Western look to it, with a preacher joining the two in holy matrimony; or, a combination service is likely. In the Shinto tradition, the main feature of the wedding ceremony is the drinking of the sake by the bride and groom from small cups, each consumed in three sips each. This solemnizes the wedding. Immediately following, a reception is held, with the bride changing attire, usually into Western dress. Family and friends take turns offering toasts of good luck, and delight in telling stories about the faults of the bride and groom. Honeymoon spots abound in Japan, and in recent years Hawaii has proved to be the number one choice for honeymooning abroad.

Defense

Since the end of World War II, the first loss to a foreign enemy and most devastating military venture in Japanese history, Japan has adopted a policy of "pacifism." Aritcle IX of the 1947 Constitution states, "The Japanese people forever renounce war as a sovereign right of the nation and the threat or use of force as a means of settling international disputes . . . land, sea and air forces . . . shall never be maintained." Japan did rearm in the 1950's despite the strong opposition which held the government decision to be unconstitutional. The Self-Defense Force, the official designation for Japan's armed forces, maintains about 250,000 troops, with an army of 13 divisions, an air force with 400 aircraft, and a navy with 50 destroyers. Under the terms of the 1960 US-Japan Treaty of Mutual Cooperation and Security, the U.S. is allowed to maintain troops in Japan, some 46,000 strong at present. By government policy, nuclear arms are neither manufactured nor maintained in Japan — the only country in the world which has suffered from nuclear attack. Japan has annually spent less than 1% of its GNP on defense since the late 1960's, in contrast to the U.S. expenditure of over 5% of its GNP. The U.S. government has been urging Japan to spend more on defense, commensurate with its strong economy. Under the present government, the defense expenditure is expected to increase; but, together with the trade imbalance problem, the defense issue is likely to remain an important factor in US-Japan relations in the foreseeable future.

Doctors And Dentists

Medical and dental standards are high in Japan and excellent medical care is available throughout the country. In Tokyo, English speaking practitioners are readily available, although less so in other parts of the country. Many of the major hotels provide clinics for their guests. The following medical centers have English speaking doctors: Hibiya Clinic, St. Luke's Hospital, Tokyo Medical and Surgical Clinic, Seventh Day Adventist Hospital, and St. Mary's Hospital. The Bluff Hospital in Yokohama, the Japan Baptist Hospital in Kyoto, and Yodogawa Christian Hospital in Osaka also provide medical assistance to the foreigner. Dental offices in Tokyo include: Otani Dental Clinic, Olympia Ohba Dental Clinic, and the Japan-American Dental Clinic. See appendix for their respective phone numbers.

E

Earthquakes

A popular notion in Japan is that an earthquake, no matter how slight, occurs somewhere every day. According to tradition, a huge catfish lies underground and the movement of the fish is what causes the tremor. Because the Japanese chain of islands is a result of volcanic action, destructive earthquakes have become commonplace throughout the country. Indeed, much of Japan lies along a number of fault lines. The most devastating earthquake in recent history occurred on September 1, 1923, causing the death of over 100,000 Tokyo residents. Most earthquakes today are only slight tremors, although seismographic records show tens of thousands of mild shocks every year.

Economy

See Also: NATURAL RESOURCES; BUSINESS IN JAPAN

The emergence of Japan as a modern state in 1868 witnessed an ability to compete in the global economy. Since the Second World War, Japan has succeeded in establishing itself as an industrial superpower. Reliant on trade to pay for its imports, its annual rate of growth from the mid-60's was approximately 10% until 1972. Since then, it has grown between 3% and 4.5% annually. In 1985 its Gross National Product (GNP) was just under two trillion dollars, about half of the U.S.'s $3.9 trillion national economy. Per capita income was close to the U.S.: $16,301 in Japan; $16,709 in the U.S. Japan's current rate of inflation is between 1% and 2% annually, which compares with the U.S.'s 1986 rate of 4%. Japan's prime lending rate is generally half that of the U.S., in recent years 3.5% vs. 7.5%, respectively. The national debt, at $520 billion, is about half that of the U.S. In 1986 unemployment was nearly 3%, while in the U.S. the year-end figure was close to a 7% national average.

Japan spends less than 1% of its GNP for defense *(q.v.)*, which is expected to increase under the present government. (The U.S. spends over 6% for defense.) Japan imports over 90% of the raw materials required to feed the nation and produce the export goods to support its economy. Yet, it imports only 22% of the industrial products it requires, while the U.S. imports 55%. In 1986, Japan exported to the U.S. some $44 billion more than America bought from Japan. This trade imbalance is seen as a major source of current U.S./Japan friction and is likely to continue in the years ahead.

Education

Emphasis on the importance of education has long been part of the Japanese tradition. In the 1870's, when the Meiji government, along with instituting educational programs aimed at modernization, decided to require four years of elementary education, this was done despite the fact that the majority of the population was already literate in reading, writing and arithmetic. In natural resource-poor Japan, an educated population may well be the most important resource of all in the production and consumption of goods and services.

The present educational system is often referred to as the 6-3-3-4 system, referring to six years of elementary school (*shogakko*), three years of middle school (*chugakko*), three years of high school (*koto gakko*), and four years of college (*daigaku*). The first nine years of education, provided without tuition costs, is compulsory. The majority of middle school graduates enroll in the high school, and about 40% of college aged youth attend a university, a comparable figure to that of the U.S.

Entrance to a university is often difficult as there are fewer openings than there are applicants, and passing an entrance examination to a prestigious university, such as the University of Tokyo or the University of Kyoto, creates keen competition. The examination is the only requirement for acceptance. In order to compete in the entrance examination, many youths attend supplementary schools, called *juku*, while they are still in elementary, middle, and high school. Many fail in the college entrance exam one or more times, and these would-be college students enroll in special preparatory schools to help themselves bone up for the next year's exam. About 75% of the entering freshman class at the University of Tokyo have spent at least one year between high school and college in such a manner, and are referred to during this period as *ronin*. (Taken from the wandering masterless samurai of feudal times.) While Japanese are rightly proud of their educational achievements, as demonstrated by one of the lowest illiteracy rates in the world, and as evidenced by consistently high performance records by high school students in science and mathematics, Japanese education is not without its problems. Emphasis on rote memory and uniformity of instruction have created a system that discourages originality and in some ways, analytical rigor. The authoritarian style of imparting knowledge has fostered the ability to absorb information, but has failed to produce many individuals with a healthy skepticism about the precepts they are exposed to; a spirit of experimentation with radically new ideas is lacking. Such is the pressure on conformity and the need to pass tests that many hopes are dashed when exams are repeatedly failed, especially when entrance to prestigious universities is at stake. It is a vulnerable time in the lives of young people and suicides associated with this failure are an ongoing concern to the society.

Electric Current

Japanese electric current is 100 volts AC, although at major hotels, outlets usually carry both 110 and 220 volts for electric appliances such as razors, hair dryers, and travel irons. Two different cycles are used: 50 cycles in eastern and northern Japan, including Tokyo; and 60 cycles in western Japan, including Nagoya, Kyoto, and Osaka. The dividing line between 50 and 60 cycles is halfway between Nagoya and Tokyo.

Emergency Information

When in Tokyo or Kyoto, English language assistance can be obtained by calling 502-1461 (Tokyo) or 371-5649 (Kyoto) from any telephone. Outside of Tokyo or Kyoto, insert a ten yen coin into any yellow or blue public telephone, and dial 106. An operator will come on the line, and by saying, "Collect call TIC," you will be connected with English speaking staff of the Tourist Information Center in either Tokyo or Kyoto. This service is available daily from 9:00 to 5:00. Another emergency service is TELL (Tokyo English Life Line): 03-264-4347, daily 9:00 to 4:00 and 7:00-11:00.

Employment

Though not always possible in small companies with fluctuating volumes of business, it is the norm of most Japanese organizations to offer lifetime employment to regular employees. When the unemployment rate exceeds 2%, as it did in the early 1980's, the nation experiences a major turmoil. (In the U.S., a 5% or 6% rate of unemployment is considered normal; in 1987, the rate was slightly over 6%.) New employees are usually recruited directly from colleges or high schools. They stay with the same company or organization until retirement. Less than half of working age women work outside their homes; most of the women who work quit their jobs when they marry or have their first child. Women who seek regular, especially professional, jobs often encounter job discrimination. Fringe benefits tend to be more generous in relative terms than those in the U.S., including health insurance and housing subsidies.

English Language

Most commentaries on the Japanese ability to speak English are unflattering. This is due to the fact that English is learned by rote memory, but not *spoken* widely. The three years of English in middle school, and the three more years in high school, emphasize the written word and composition skills development. Conversation is lacking, owing to the teacher's poor pronunciation and marginal ability to speak English. Even in the universities, where English is again required, the emphasis is on memorization to pass tests and the texts used are very difficult. In recent years, the Japanese have increased their efforts to learn English, especially listening comprehension. They have a great financial and ego investment. The most proficient are those who have gone abroad to study. As a result, the Japanese language is replete with English language "loan words." A native English speaker can usually land a job teaching English in Japan. There is a national commitment, from the highest levels on down, to learning practical English because of its role as an international means of communication. It would be hard to find a nation spending more with less results. On those rare occasions when a foreigner is approached by an unknown Japanese, English will invariably be spoken, and the foreigner will assume it is Japanese that is being spoken. Learning to understand the Japanese pronunciation of English is a constructive step in attempting to communicate in Japan. Speaking English slowly, with a slight Japanese accent, will also facilitate the conversation when the foreign visitor knows no Japanese.

Entertainment
See Also: BARS; RESTAURANTS; THEATER
According to prevailing custom, official entertainment in Japan is generally only for men. Rarely does a Japanese man invite his wife along when entertaining a guest, foreigners included, unless the man is traveling with a wife or companion. Japanese consider it a burden on the guest to tell him all about what they will do in an evening, and so, unlike business schedules, the social schedule is not written out or explained beforehand.

In response to entertainment customs abroad, some changes, such as including wives and invitations to homes, are beginning to be seen. For those on their own, whether in a group or alone, there is a variety of entertainment available, especially in the larger cities, including Tokyo, Osaka, Kyoto, Kobe, Yokohama, and others. The list seems endless: night spots for dinner and a show, or dinner and dancing, or just dancing; live shows, including revues, musicals, ballet, modern dance; *kabuki*; *noh*; concerts and recitals of traditional and Western classical/popular music; roadshow and revival movies, both Japanese and foreign; puppet theater; modern theater; exhibits, in galleries, department stores, museums; tours on the town, day or night; sports — and more, including a circus now and again. Most events start early, often before six, and end around ten at night, allowing commuters to catch the last train home.

F

Family

Despite the fact that geographical mobility has increased tremendously in the post World War II period, families in Japan have, in general, remained close-knit. The oldest married son (if there is no male child, the oldest daughter) and his wife (or her husband) and children usually live with the aging parents, making three-generation families a very common arrangement. Divorces occur in fewer than one out of 6 marriages. Emotional bonds between family members are strong, and a family as a whole tends to act as a collective decision-making unit in economic and sociological terms. Japanese family structure and sentiment found within them have often been compared with traditional Italian and Jewish families. When the musical "Fiddler on the Roof" was performed in Tokyo several years ago, one Japanese critic wondered how Americans could appreciate it, since it is so "Japanese." When family members are scattered, it is customary that they get together at least twice a year, once for the New Year's celebration, and the other for *Obon* (See Festivals) in midsummer.

Festivals
See Also: NATIONAL HOLIDAYS

Widely celebrated festivals, but not national holidays, include the following *matsuri* and the dates on which they are observed:

FEBRUARY 3/4.   *Setsubun* (Bean-throwing ritual). Observed at shrines, temples, and in the home, people cast little red beans and shout, *"Fuku wa uchi; oni wa soto."* This means: "Happiness, in. Evil spirits, out!"

APRIL 8.   Buddha's birthday, also known as *"hana matsuri."* Floats are decorated for parades to the temples, and sweet tea is used to refresh the icons of Buddhism within the temple environs. Fresh flowers are offered to the images in the home and in the temples.

MAY 1.   May Day. Part of Golden Week, which begins with the Emperor's birthday on April 29. The unions, Communists, and Socialists celebrate the day with marches, picnics, and political speeches.

31

JULY 7.	Tanabata Festival (See Tanabata).
JULY 15.	*Obon*, or All Souls Festival. In some regions of the country, this festival is celebrated on or about August 15, partly due to observance of the festival in accordance with the lunar calendar, partly due to the farmers freer schedule in August. Fires are lit, people dance in the street or temple yards, wearing *yukata kimono*, on behalf of their deceased ancestors. It is a time of joy and all-night merrymaking. The dance music is provided by young drummers and flute players who are situated on a stand raised high above the crowds who dance around them. The lights serve to show the spirits of the dead the way back to their former homes for a brief "visit."
NOVEMBER 15.	*Shichi-go-san* ("7-5-3"). Girls aged seven or three, and boys of five, are escorted to the shrine to thank the *"ubusama"* or guardian deity for their safe upbringing thus far in life. Traditional kimono are worn by girls and their mothers, while the boys and fathers may wear suits. Parents rival each other in attempting to outdress their children. It is the highlight of the fall festivals, and dates from the Tokugawa era.
DECEMBER 24.	Christmas Eve (See Christmas).
DECEMBER 31.	New Year's Eve (See New Year).

Films

Tokyo is one of the film capitals of the world. The nation's leading studios, Nikkatsu, Toei, Shochiku, and Toho are located there, and since the early fifties, these and other lesser studios have helped Japan compete both in terms of quantity and quality in world cinematic activity. Beginning with *Rashomon*, a host of Japanese movies have won coveted prizes and lifted Japanese films in the eyes of foreigners and Japanese alike. Today, movie houses number in the thousands, and about one third of the movies shown are from abroad. Those from America, France, England, Germany, and Italy are chief among them. Invariably, the original sound track is retained, and the Japanese subtitles appear on the right side of the screen. The Japanese movie is popular abroad, as well, and the samurai film is foremost. Comparable to the "Western" in the U.S., the *"chanbara"* films provide release through heroism, action, violence, and romance. Kyoto, the second largest film-making center in Japan, provides a good background for period movies. Movie houses are clean, comfortable, and often crowded; road shows command top money for admission.

Flower Arranging

The art of flower arranging (*Ikebana*) dates from the Muromachi era. Natural flowers, in all their grace and beauty, are brought into the home, and placed in the *tokonoma* (alcove) or other locations in the home. The shape and color of the flower suggests to the practitioner the use of minimal branches and other material in achieving a simplicity of form. There are many schools of arrangement, one of the leading of which is the Ikenobo, the name of an early Kyoto master of the art.

Folk Dance

Modern folk dance in Japan finds its roots in the earliest forms of religious rites and stage arts. One of these styles is the *bugaku* which is still danced at the Imperial Palace. Today's folk dances draw from the traditions that have formed the *Noh* and *Kabuki*, as well as the Geisha dances which are performed much as they always have been. Most folk dances have religious significance, whether Shinto or Buddhist. There are dances for rice planting, rain-invoking, harvests and other similar occasions. Most of the festivals have their special dances, including the All Souls Festival (*o-bon*), New Years, Tanabata, etc. There are dances to bring good luck, scare away devils, and to purify sites. Many dances, performed by groups, are like a parade as they move along; still others are performed on stage or, if outdoors, in a contained area. Some dances are performed by musicians, while others keep the dancers and musicians separate. Places to see folk dances abound in the larger cities. In Kyoto, the Gion Corner, catering to the foreign tourist, has a selection of dances and drama, along with other traditional performing arts.

Food And Drink

In the major urban centers, such as Tokyo and Osaka, there is a wide variety of restaurants serving food suitable for every mood and palate. In addition to a whole host of Japanese foods, one can expect excellent French, German, Chinese, and Russian foods. Each of the major hotels in these cities will offer a choice of Western or Japanese food. The following are typical Japanese dishes:

Beverages

Sake heads the list of traditional Japanese drinks. It is the rice wine that has become the national drink. It is made (and consumed) all over Japan, but finds its origins and best distilleries in the Kobe area. *Shochu* is the working man's stronger version, and it is mixed with yeast and other ingredients as a staple in cooking, where it is called *mirin*.

The major beer producers in Japan are Asahi, Kirin, Sapporo, and Suntory. Beer is sold widely in bottles, cans and at dispensing machines. Whiskeys are produced by Suntory and Nikka (mostly scotch). Japanese are fond of Western wine, and grow grapes (in the Kofu area near Tokyo) which form the basis for expanding domestic enterprise. There are a variety of soft drinks, in domestic brands and imports, such as Coke. Fresh and canned juices are universally available. As a thirst quencher, Japanese prefer green tea, served free of charge, and automatically, at restaurants. Tea comes in all grades, and the thickest is reserved for the tea ceremony. Coffee is widely available, particularly at the ubiquitous *kissaten* (See Tea House).

Kaiseki
Perhaps the most formal of all Japanese meals, and one which appeals as much to the visual senses as to its subtleties of taste, is the *Kaiseki ryori*. It is a very delicate multi-course meal composed of seasonal fish or vegetables. The presentation, usually on *tatami* in a *ryokan* or in the *zashiki* area of a restaurant, is an end in itself. Carefully chosen plates and bowls, all in harmony with each other and the surroundings, allow for the meal to proceed according to an elaborate scenario: appetizers, clear soups, raw fish, boiled and then fried dishes, followed by a main dish of fish or fowl, then rice and pickles, the traditional ending of the formal meal. Fruit may follow as a dessert.

Sashimi
This is sushi without rice; raw fish traditionally prepared. It is often served as an hors d'oeuvre to many of the described dishes.

Shabu-Shabu
Similar to sukiyaki in ingredients, the thin slices of beef are cooked along with the vegetables in a broth, creating a soup-like dish. The ingredients are eaten one at a time, and the meal is topped off with the broth into which noodles or rice is placed. When chicken is used instead of beef, the dish is called *Mizutaki*.

Sukiyaki
Thinly sliced beef is cooked in an iron pan with vegetables, bean curd, and vermicelli. Whether served in a restaurant or at home, the meal is cooked in front of the guests. Water, *sake*, and a little sugar is added to form the broth. When complete, the sukiyaki is placed in a small bowl which has a beaten raw egg in it. This serves as a coolant to the hot dish, and adds considerably to the taste.

Sushi
This is a cold dish composed of oval shaped rice balls topped by a piece of fresh uncooked fish, usually tuna, cuttlefish, or shrimp. Certain sushi are wrapped in seaweed and the center has cucumber, pickled radish, or a combination of these and fish. A sweetened egg omelet is another variation. It is customary to eat sushi with the fingers, dipping it along with pickled ginger, into soy sauce.

Tempura

Shrimp, seasonal fish, vegetables, and dried seaweed are some of the ingredients used. Each are dipped in a batter and then fried in vegetable oil. Because tempura is best when eaten hot, Japanese enjoy sitting at a tempura bar, where the food is prepared and served at once.

Tonkatsu

This is a popular pork dish, breaded and served with rice and cut cabbage. When placed directly on the rice, and onions and egg are added, it is known as *Katsudon*. *Katsu* is English (cuts). *Don* is short for *domburi*, the bowl.

Other favorite foods include *kushiage*, or foods deep fried on a skewer; beef, chicken, pork, fish, vegetables in combination are prepared this way. *Yakitori*, or barbecued chicken, is also on skewers, and served as an hors d'oeuvre or late snack. Snacks can be purchased on the street from vendors who, according to their specialty, may also serve *oden*. *Oden* is sold at stalls on cold winter nights and goes well with sake. The vendor cooks pieces of *tofu, taro, fish sausage (kamaboko)* and *konnyaku* (noodles made of devils-tongue) in a large pan. *Soba* and *udon* are Japanese noodles, made from buckwheat flour and wheat flour, respectively. They are served in a broth, piping hot and well-seasoned. These are dishes popular with the common folk, and are taken as light meals or late night snacks.

Fuji

Mt. Fuji (*Fujiyama* or *Fuji-san*) is Japan's tallest mountain and highest elevation (12,388 ft.). It is visible to the southwest on clear days from Tokyo, located within a few hours train ride. Its setting is ideal, surrounded by five lakes and nestled between the sea and other less imposing mountains. Long held sacred, the mountain is referred to in works of art and poetry as the symbol of a country unified (*fu-ji* can also mean "indivisible"). Fuji is snow-capped most of the year, and there is only about a month when climbers can reach the top; and it is the ambition of all Japanese to reach the top once in a lifetime to see the magic rays of the morning sun above the clouds. A popular saying warns, "It is as foolish not to climb Mt. Fuji as it is to climb it twice."

Funerals

A funeral is one of the most important family functions in Japan. Although there are regional variations, the funeral is typically performed according to the Buddhist rites. The custom of cremation is as old as the Buddhist tradition, which requires the presence of a priest to chant over the prepared body which is dressed in white and annointed with aromatics. Members of the family, relatives and friends gather together in a ceremony known as *otsuya* — "passing the night." Incense is burned and offering made as the priest chants from the scriptures. Family and guests make gifts for the dead, and in turn are served food and drink. Traditionally, these rites take place in the home, after which the funeral procession proceeds to the crematorium. After cremation, the deceased's ashes are placed in an urn in a family designated area of a graveyard plot. The rites continue for many days after this. On the anniversary date of the death, the family visits the grave site and children report their progress to those who have died before them.

Furoshiki

A very handy oversized wrapping cloth with many uses in Japan, originally used to carry fresh clothes to the bath (*o-furo*). The daily life of the Japanese, particularly women, would not be as efficient without them. They fold up neatly and tidily until needed. When a purchase is made, it serves as a wrap around to facilitate carrying, and to add color to the shopping experience. The *furoshiki* come in many sizes and colors. The designs that are placed on every kind of fabric, from silk to cotton, are indications of the intended use. From functional use, such as carrying office workers' lunches, children's textbooks, or vegetables, to taking gifts to friends, the *furoshiki* has come a long way, but is still used from time to time as a bath spread.

Futon

Japanese bedding, laid directly onto the *tatami* floor, is universally used as both bed and bed clothes. There is an increased use of the futon on Western-style beds, but the function is the same. Introduced from China by Japanese Buddhist priests who studied there in the 10th Century, the futon serves a functional role and consists of two oblong coverings stuffed with cotton. The flatter and heavier of the two is the *shiki-buton* used for the bottom mattress; the *kake-buton* is placed over the top as the cover. Futon come in kimono-like patterns and colors, and usually have fitted sheets which can be removed and washed. They are aired during the day along the veranda of the house, or over the railing of the apartment sun porch.

G

Gaijin

Short for *gaikokujin*, meaning "outsider" or "foreigner." It does not necessarily have pejorative connotations. Americans and Europeans are most likely referred to, or addressed, as *gaijin* or *gaijin-san*. Even though *gaikokujin* literally refers to any non-Japanese and is used as such in official documents, the popular usage limits its reference only to non-Oriental foreigners.

Games

See Also: SPORTS

Use of leisure time in Japan has increased recently, with many companies and government agencies moving to a five-day week. Much of the free time is spent watching television or engaging in sports. However, traditional games still have a firm place in the Japanese recreational schedule. Some of the more popular ones include:

Card Games

The following card games remain popular:
Karuta (from "card"): The *utagaruta*, or *hyakunin-isshu*, are poem cards with selections from 100 poets. The object is to hear part of the poem recited, and then find the card which completes the poem. The person who collects the most cards wins the game. *Iroha karuta*, or alphabet cards, played by children, is similar to *utagaruta*, but the poems used begin with a different symbol of the phonetic script; the game stimulates reading skills. The *hanafuda*, or flower cards, can be learned by the foreigner who has not yet learned to read Japanese. It uses 48 cards depicting flowers and seasonal phenomena. The rules resemble poker.

Go

Believed to be the oldest game in the world, Japanese claim this as their national game. Although the Chinese were playing Go centuries before Christ, the Japanese have outplayed their Chinese counterparts since shortly after the game's introduction in the 8th Century. Like other games and sports, a strict ranking system is in effect. The highest attainable individual rank is "9" — and few, probably less than a dozen, have reached that pinnacle.

The Go board is a solid block of sturdy wood about 17 x 16 inches square. Nineteen black lines crisscross to form 361 intersections. Three hundred and sixty-one black and white stones are used (black outnumbers white by one). The black stones are given to the under-dog who gets the first move. The object of the game is to gain territory by surrounding the opponent's stones, removing them from action. Go typically lasts one or two hours.

Mahjong

A mild form of gambling, *mah-jong* is for the marathon game player. Much like gin rummy in its essence, the game is played by four persons who sit around a table on which the tiles lie, either face up, or stacked for one's eyes only in front of each player. One to two hour bouts of *mah-jong* are strung together and can last all night. The game's enjoyment stems from the strategies and conspiracies to win, and from the conversations that provide much-needed relaxation for businessmen. *Mah-jong* was introduced from China by way of the U.S.

Pachinko

Pachinko parlors are curious sights to first-time visitors to Japan. In most cities of any size, these arcades are not easy to miss: neon-lit rooms with loud music and prizes stacked in the windows attract the idle and overworked slaves of modern industry. *Pachinko* gets its name from the sound of the little steel balls as they hit the pins. Like a vertical pinball machine, the operator becomes mesmerized by the action, which is fast paced and lucrative for the skilled. Originally manually operated (it's a post-war phenomenon), *pachinko* has now gone electrical. Skill is still required, because the control device is like a joy stick on a video game and requires hand-eye coordination.

Shogi

Perhaps the most popular of the games played on a board. Its origin seems to be Persian, and *shogi* are "pawns of the shah." Like chess, the objective is to get the opposing king with the use of twenty men set up in three rows. There are 81 squares and the battle scene varies somewhat from chess: captured players can be used by the opponent; some eighty moves are required to complete the game; *shogi* men are five-sided flat slabs with their names written in Chinese characters. *Shogi* tips appear in daily newspapers, and the highest ranking *shogi* players are prominent members of society.

Geisha

A *geisha* is a "talented person." More specifically, a woman entertainer who is a specialist in song and dance. Located in the larger urban centers, such as Tokyo, Kyoto, and Osaka, *geisha* have for centuries catered to the needs of the tired businessman or self-indulgent sons (and fathers) of noble houses. With glossy black hair (now, usually a wig), the *geisha* is conspicuously attired in gay kimono, brocaded *obi* (sash), and excessive makeup. Kyoto is the training center, and the younger apprentice girls from age ten to sixteen are called *maiko*. *Geisha* are expected to return the cost of their training to the mistresses of the establishments which hire them. This may take a lifetime or, if the *geisha* is beautiful, her debts may be paid outright by some wealthy man who fancies her for his wife or mistress. *Geisha* are schooled in the fine arts of singing, dancing, *shamisen* playing, and flower arranging.

Geography

See Also: SPECIFIC GEOGRAPHIC AREAS, e.g. HONSHU, TOKYO, ETC.

Japan is made up of four principal islands, Hokkaido (q.v.), Honshu (q.v.), Kyushu (q.v.), and Shikoku (q.v.). These and thousands of lesser islands form an arc, east of the Asian land mass, which comprises 142,726 square miles and stretches in a north to southwesterly direction. The total land mass is 1/25th the size of the United States, and would fit entirely within the state of California. Between the latitudinal zones of 27° N. and 45° N. the oceanic island setting places Japan in an invigorating climate. Japan is one of the first countries in the international time zone. Physical features of the country derive from the volcanic and earthquake activity which have sculpted the face of the landscape, 75% of which is mountainous. Short and rapid rivers and natural lakes abound and add to the scenic splendor. Plains and other flat basins and tablelands account for only one-fifth of the land space. The arable soil, including the major human settlements, comprises less than 15% of the total land area.

The mountains are linked by chains, the most spectacular of which are the Japan Alps in central, northern, and southern Honshu. The tallest mountain is Fuji (*q.v.*). The lengthy and varied coastline of 16,470 miles helps account for Japan's emergence as a fishing and maritime power.

Gestures

See Also: BOWING

There are several distinct gestures which need to be clearly understood, although it may be unnecessary or impractical for non-Japanese to use them.

- A circle made by the thumb and index finger refers to money — not to be interpreted as a sign for "okay."

- A raised thumb refers to one's boss or "old man"; not a symbol for "right on."

- A raised little finger refers to a "girl friend," "mistress," or "wife."

- A circling motion with the index finger near one's ear indicates that one thinks the person under discussion is insane. This is very strong "language" and, as such, should not be used or taken lightly.

39

- The typical way a Japanese indicates "oneself" is to point the right index finger at one's nose. Pointing to one's heart with the entire hand indicates "confidence."

- A thumb placed between the index finger and middle finger refers to the sexual act, or female organ. The American children's game, "I got your nose!" should not be played in Japan.

- The open right hand moving up and down rapidly with the thumb close to the nose indicates, "excuse me," and is used especially when one must cross another's path, or must walk in such a way as to block the view of others.

- A stretched right arm held horizontally with the hand facing downward, waving inward from the wrist, means "come here."

- A tapping together of the right and left index fingers so as they cross, refers to a "fight" or "strained personal relations." This gesture simulates a sword fight.

- A hooked index finger refers to someone's "crookedness," or a "thief."

- There are three gestures the Japanese use, for the most part unconsciously, which indicate awkwardness, hesitation, dismay or predicament:
    Inhaling air audibly through clenched teeth.
    Scratching the back of one's head.
    Hitting lightly against the forehead with one's open palm.

- Moving the open hand across one's chest or face in a fanning motion signifies "no," "don't do it," "not for me," or "I don't understand."

- Silence is not a gesture in a strict sense, but is used by Japanese in different ways and often signifies things other than what Americans might interpret it to mean. Silence *per se* is not a sign of negative or hostile feelings. It is often employed deliberately to indicate thoughtfulness and quiet appreciation. A "wise" person in Japan is supposed to speak slowly, quietly, and with many pauses.

- Laughing and smiling also at times indicate sentiments other than humor or joy. Sadness, confusion, or embarrassment may all be expressed by Japanese laughter. If a Japanese person laughs when the situation is not funny, it is best not to laugh along, or to question, "What is funny?"

Geta And Zori

Geta are wooden clogs, and *zori* are sandals, or thongs. Both are footwear and are normally worn with traditional Japanese dress. *Geta* today are much like they have been for centuries, perhaps a little shorter in height and a little longer, especially for women, whose feet are generally larger than they were in the Edo period. *Geta* are worn with *yukata* or summer *kimono*, and *zori* are worn with the formal attire. Many *zori* owned by wealthy women are coordinated with the many styles and colors of their expensive kimonos.

Gifts And Giving

Besides gift giving on personal occasions, such as births, graduations, and weddings, the Japanese have many well-established and elaborate customs concerning gift giving. Some major categories are as follows:

Chugen and Seibo: Shortly before *Obon* in mid-summer and at the year-end, subordinates give gifts to their superiors, companies to their clients, and, sometimes, stores to their major customers. The summer gift is called *Chugen*, the winter's, *Seibo*. The gifts for these occasions are usually liquor and cured food items, such as salted salmon for *Seibo*.

Koden: The monetary gift that one brings to a funeral. It is given in a special envelope.

Omiyage: Literally meaning "local product," this is the gift to bring home when returning from a trip, or to bring to someone one is visiting (including a business client) in a distant place.

Senbetsu: A person leaving on a long journey receives money from relatives and friends. In turn, the person will return with *omiyage* for those relatives and friends.

Tsukaimono: Japanese almost never visit someone's home without taking at least a small gift, called "*tsukaimono*" ("things to use").

By American standards, the Japanese often appear to give extravagant gifts to a wide range of people. Sometimes, the gifts are given under circumstances which may, to Americans, look like bribery. Gift giving, however, has been an important factor in cultivating, and negotiating with, business clients in Japan; the custom does not seem to be changing.

Ginza

The most popular street in Tokyo, and the bustling shopping center which stretches for a dozen or so blocks between Shimbashi on the southern end and Nihombashi on the north. The name comes from the silver mint which was opened in the area in 1612. The Ginza was the first street in Japan with pavement and brick houses lining the way. Today the smartest shops and the major department stores are located within walking distance of each other. Walking is associated with the Ginza; "*gimbura*" is a stroll, and a walker's paradise is open every Sunday. Auto traffic is closed and the entire stretch is devoted to relaxation and strolling up and down the avenue. The heart of the Ginza is the intersection at 4-chome, with the Mitsukoshi and Wako department stores competing with the San-Ai building as the most prestigious and expensive real estate in Japan.The Imperial grounds are nearby, and in the opposite direction, the theater district, where the Kabukiza is the centerpiece.

Government

See Also: POLITICS

The post World War II Constitution which went into effect on May 3, 1947, remaining unamended to date, stipulates the basic structure of government. The three main branches of government are legislative, executive, and judicial. The executive branch is answerable to the legislative body, making the Japanese structure more similar to the British parliamentary system than to that of the U.S. Any Japanese citizen over the age of 20 has the right to vote in the Diet (legislative body) elections, as well as in local elections. Basic human rights, such as equality of sex and freedom of assembly and expression, are guaranteed under the Constitution. Japan is a unitary state; its forty-seven prefectures do not enjoy autonomous power like that of American states in the federal system. Traffic laws and laws governing business activities or education are uniform throughout the country.

Groups

The group orientation of the Japanese and the individualist orientation of Americans are perhaps the most dissimilar cultural traits found between the two societies. The Japanese are far more likely to conceive their material and emotional well-being as stemming from their association with a group — be it a family, company, or school. Individual ingenuity, diligence and courage, Americans tend to believe, are what eventually produce progress and prosperity in society. Japanese tend to believe that collective effort and cooperation in a group eventually produce happiness for each individual member of that group. When group consciousness is as supreme as it is in Japan, harmony (*wa*) among the members of the group is often regarded as more important than individual rights or interests. Group activities and conformity to group norms are constantly encouraged from childhood throughout adult life. One of the most conspicuous group activities is sightseeing. It is rare indeed to see a lone Japanese tourist — especially abroad.

Hakone

A year-round resort near Mt. Fuji, popular with foreigners as well as Japanese and easily accessible from Tokyo. Bus and train service is available, and a good set of roads makes the trip by auto a pleasure if the roads are not congested. Hot springs resorts, many with their special view of Fuji, provide one of the best spots to try out a Japanese inn. The leading lake in the area is Ashi, and the variety of shrines, temples, mountains, trees, and other attractions, natural as well as manmade, offer a welcome retreat from Tokyo's concrete and steel in a matter of a few hours.

Haragei

Alluding to "mind art," the term refers to a style of personal interaction without the use of words. It is akin to communicating through the process of intuition, reflected in "gut feelings," and is more often resorted to by Japanese as a device for acting out or performing one's intentions than the more explicit methods generally used in America. For example, when negotiating a price in a business deal, the use of *haragei* makes it possible for the buyer to hint at what is a good price, without actually saying so; the seller conjectures about what the buyer is able to pay, and the final quotation is based on this indirect process of using tangential data, even moods, to communicate one's desires. Because it is based on implied conditions which are mutually understood, both parties use *haragei* to fashion a proper understanding, without stating something bluntly or directly.

Hiroshima

About two and a half hours by air from Tokyo (or five hours by Bullet Train), lying southwest of Tokyo, Hiroshima is the prefectural capital of Hiroshima-ken, and the heart of the Chugoku district of Japan. The name derives from the delta — Broad Island. Today this city of over 730,000 is the third largest urban center west of Kobe. On August 6, 1945, at 8:15 a.m., Hiroshima was completely flattened by the atom bomb. Over 200,000 people died as a result. In the center of the city, on the site of the blast's epicenter, a museum and memorial ground are dedicated to the theme of "No more Hiroshimas." Nearby sites include the reconstructed castle; Miyajima (Itsukushima Shrine); and Kintaibashi, the "floating bridge."

History

The major periods of Japanese history are: (1) Prehistory — the mythological era including the establishment of the country (? to 600 A.D.); (2) Imperial State and Nara Period (600 to 784); (3) Heian Period — the development of court aristocracy (794 to 1192); (4) Kamakura Period — introduction of feudalism (1192 to 1333); (5) Muromachi and Azuchi-Momoyama Periods — the civil wars dominate (1333 to 1599); (6) Edo or Tokugawa Period — time of unification (1600 to 1867); (7) Meiji Era — restoration of Imperial rule and development of modern state (1868 to 1912); (8) Taisho and early Showa Eras — rise and fall of Imperialist Japan (1912 to 1945); (9) Post World War II — period of recovery and emergence as economic superpower.

The Japanese are strongly aware of their history. Many of the customs observed and values held today derive from the earliest times. Behavior and attitudes of modern Japanese find their roots in many of the feudal period concepts and values transmitted to society through art, literature, and education. The country was isolated from cultures other than Chinese and Korean throughout most of its early history, hence, Buddhism and Confucianism are the early shapers. Western technology and institutions formed the second wave of influence prior to the expansionist activity leading to the Second World War. Before 1945, Japan had never lost a war or been conquered.

Ancient Japanese, dating from Neolithic times, grouped themselves into family communities (*Uji*). The dominant *Uji* combined to form a unified state as early as the 4th Century. Mythology and Chinese influence in keeping records provide the only history of early life in Japan, and are sketchy and unreliable. These records, known as the *Kojiki* and *Nihongi* (both are records of ancient activities), outline the development of Japan and were probably influenced by the Chinese and Korean families who introduced writing, religion, political organization, and other major influences into the islands. In early evidence, and still visible today, is the Japanese tendency towards adopting and adapting foreign ideas and ways. Inported technologies and notions have rarely escaped the modification process peculiar to the Japanese, and the obviousness of the process suggests one element of the historical personality: the collective approach to the improvement of the Japanese way of life.

Hokkaido

Japan's second largest island, Hokkaido, is the northernmost of the four major islands. To the north lies the Okhotsk Sea; to the east, the Pacific Ocean. The Japan Sea lies to the west, and to the south, the Tsugaru Straits separate Hokkaido from Honshu, the main island. Although Hokkaido comprises 22% of the total land area of Japan, only 5% of the population (more than 5,250,000 people) live there. The seat of local government is located in Sapporo. Typical of the scenery are volcanic mountains, clear lakes, thick forests, and extensive fertile land. Five national parks located in Hokkaido are especially popular with tourists: Daisetsuzan, Akan, Shikotsu-Toya, Rishiri-Rebun-Sarobetsu, and Shiretoko Hakodate. Otaru and Muroran are seaports; Asahikawa is a thriving urban center second only to Sapporo in size. Between Muroran and Sapporo is one of Japan's most famous spas, Noboribetsu. The hot springs are so plentiful that a variety of baths can be taken at most of the inns in the resort. Nearby Shiraoi is the home of some 700 *Ainu* (*q.v.*).

Honshu

The main island on which are located the principal cities and regions of Japan. It occupies 61% of the total land area of Japan. The island is divided into five districts; from north to south, they are: Tohoku, Kanto, Chubu, Kinki, and Chugoku. The Kanto area is the primary seat of government, business and academia. Honshu is larger than England, Scotland, and Wales combined. A mountain chain traverses the entire length of Honshu; the result is that Honshu is divided into major geograhical areas, differing in customs, climate, and regional identity. Thirty-four of the forty-seven prefectures are located on Honshu.

Hotels

There are a variety of accommodations in Japan, varying in price and style. The Western-style hotels frequented by foreigners are of generally good quality, and the major hotels are of the highest standards and offer full services. Reservations can be made through an airline, an agent, or a chain/affiliate hotel. Prices for single rooms vary from a low of ¥4000 to a high of ¥25,000. Doubles or twins range from the mid ¥6000 to ¥45,000. Meals are separate, and the average prices are: Breakfast ¥1250; lunch ¥2500; and dinner ¥4000.

Although there are dozens of Western-style hotels in Japan, only a few can be classed as "major" — that is, providing the full array of services mentioned in this book regarding food, lodging, English language interpretation/translation, bookstores, medical and pharmaceutical services, travel arrangements for local-national-international tours, meeting rooms, and shopping arcades. A listing of above average hotels in Tokyo and Osaka and their phone numbers can be found in the appendix.

Reservations must be made well in advance to assure space. This can be done before arrival, through airlines or travel agents.

If the hotel charge per person per night is under ¥5,000, no tax is assessed. A 10 per cent tax is imposed on amounts above this, including food and drinks.

Japanese-style inns, or *ryokan*, are often quaint enterprises with an attractive entrance and someone there to greet guests and take their

45

shoes before they enter. Slippers are worn to the room, where the guests find *tatami* flooring, *yukata kimono*, and possibly *geta* (*q.v.*) waiting for them. Although many Western-style hotels have Japanese rooms, the flavor of the *ryokan* is missing. Many *ryokan* have a large, public bath as well as small, more private bathing areas.

Ryokan charges per person are more expensive than hotels, but include at least one meal, often breakfast. A 10 to 15% tax is included in the bill.

Foreign visitors may wish to stay at the very inexpensive "business hotels," which offer "no frills" services. The rooms are small, simple, and cost on the average, ¥5000 a night. Still other facilities for lodging include youth hotels, and peoples' inns (*kokumin shukusha*), but they are rarely used by foreigners not on very tight budgets.

I

Ikebukuro

This "suburb" of Tokyo has developed into one of the busiest sectors of the greater metropolitan area. A transportation hub for many private lines, such as Seibu and Tobu lines, and subways, the Japan National Railways also stops along its circle line (Yamate) around the city. Ikebukuro has grown up around the station, and now boasts one of Japan's largest buildings, the Sunshine City complex. It is the home of Rikkyo University (St. Paul's), a private school operated by the Episcopalian Church. Lafcadio Hearn, the great interpreter of things Japanese, is buried in the Zoshigaya cemetery, not far from which is the Sugamo Prison, where General Tojo and other war criminals were incarcerated.

Interpreting And Translation Service

Many foreigners who visit Japan, on business or as tourists, find a need for interpreting (spoken language) and translation (written language) assistance. While the Japanese appear to understand what is being spoken, or written, owing to a long-time investment in the study of English, many, especially the elderly, cannot speak or understand English. If one desires to communicate efficiently and accurately, a reliable interpreter or translator is a must. If the foreigner is the one seeking to do business, the burden may be on him or her to find assistance. Even when the English of the Japanese persons with whom one is dealing in a formal manner is "good," it may either be considered impolite to put the onus of language on others, or impractical. The foreign negotiator is at a distinct disadvantage if the interpretation/translation is paid for by the Japanese. There may very well be a greater loyalty to the employer in this case.

Excellent translation and interpretation services can be found in major cities, often available in large hotels. See the appendix for a listing of these services in Tokyo.

J

JIS Mark

A design based on the three initial letters of Japan Industrial Standards. The design appears on many manufactured goods made in Japan and indicates the product's compliance with standards which facilitate interchangeability of parts. It is a coveted mark, as it carries with it an implicit seal of government approval. There are other marks, especially dealing with the safety of products, which are placed on items that have passed rigid performance or inspection standards, such as food and drug products. Further, some marks appear on consumer products which guarantee producer liability in the event of injury caused by the use of the product. Claims are facilitated when the product in question bears a safety mark. American and European manufacturers have recently succeeded in gaining access to the JIS and other marks for some of the goods they export to Japan. JIS marks are difficult to obtain, owing to complex testing procedures, and Japan's insistence on the highest technical standards.

K

Kabuki

The stage art of Japan which has three hundred years of tradition behind its unique use of men in all of the roles. Although originated in the 17th Century by a woman, named Okuni, *Kabuki* was soon prohibited by law due to the deterioration of public morals attributed to her all-woman troupe. *Kabuki* thereafter developed into a rich and colorful tradition with men so convincingly playing women's parts that, today, their gestures and language are studied by women eager to improve on feminine mannerisms. A major influence in the *Kabuki* has been *Bunraku* (q.v.), with free borrowing of techniques, music, singing, dancing, and scenery. The puppet ballad has accounted for much of the stylized movements of *Kabuki*. Themes of the *Kabuki* plays, which can last up to six hours at a time, are feudalistic in setting and sentiment. Loyalty, love, sacrifice, revenge, conflicts between clans and individuals — these are the contents of *Kabuki* drama even today. The Kabukiza, east of the Ginza (*q.v.*), and the National Theater, near the Imperial Palace, provide the two major facilities for *Kabuki* performances in Tokyo.

Kamakura

Located one hour from Tokyo by train, Kamakura is a quiet seaside city which is a popular bedroom community for people who work in Yokohama and Tokyo. It is also a tourist resort, and the nearby beach and recreation facilities attract summer visitors from greater Tokyo. For foreign visitors, the Great Buddha (*Daibutsu*) is of particular interest. The bronze sitting figure of Amitabha (Amida in Japanese) is 38 ft. high and has been on an open site since 1369. The Tsurugaoka Hachimangu Shrine is the other major site of Kamakura. Its setting, the grounds and buildings, and the "National Treasures" contained within are especially attractive during the annual festival of the shrine on September 15 and 16. For the temple and shrine enthusiast, there are 65 Buddhist temples and 19 Shinto shrines in Kamakura. Many artists and novelists live there, as did the late Kawabata Yasunari, Nobel laureate author.

Keidanren

The Keizai Dantai Rengo Kai, shortened to "Keidanren," is the Federation of Economic Organizations. It is composed of the major industrial and financial organizations of Japan. It began in 1945 in an attempt to reorganize the shattered war-torn economy. It has remained as the largest federation of various Japanese industrial organizations, and includes the manufacturing, banking and finance, insurance, trade, transportation, and agricultural sectors of private industry. Two other leading federations are the Management Association of Japan (Keizai Doyukai) and the Japan Federation of Employers Associations (Nikkeiren).

Kobe

Three and a half hours southwest of Tokyo, along the Tokaido, and accessible by train or auto expressway, Kobe is the prefectural seat of Hyogo. Kobe — "God's doorway" — is, as a thriving seaport, the area's counterpart of Yokohama. Inhabited by some 1.5 million people, it spreads along the seacoast as part of a metropolitan corridor comprised of Osaka, Ashiya and Nishinomiya. The long chain of nearby mountains, Rokkozan, provides splendid views and appropriate settings for homes of wealthy merchants. One of the locally made foods, "Kobe sembei," is a sweet Japanese cracker. It is purchased as a souvenir to take back home by those visiting the area.

Kyoto

From 794 to 1868, Kyoto was the capital of Japan. For more than ten centuries it was the center of Japan's civilization and government, and still remains the cultural capital and education center of western Japan today.

To most foreigners, it is the most important place to visit in Japan. With a population of approximately 1,500,000, Kyoto is Japan's fifth largest city. A modern urban area which manages to retain its old world character and human charm, it is nestled between the Higashiyama mountains to the east, and Arashiyama to the west. There are over 1500 Buddhist temples and 200 Shinto shrines; clearly, it is the center of Buddhism with some thirty sect headquarters located in the city. Kyoto sits on a flat plain of some 385 square miles; it enjoys a mild climate, but has four distinct seasons which bring splendor to the thousands of gardens with their variety of flowers, trees and shrubs.

Just seven minutes under three hours (exactly) by Bullet Train from Tokyo, the city offers a look at traditional Japan come to life. There are several city-wide festivals each month of the year, and the sightseeing opportunities are inexhaustible. One-day tours to Nara from Kyoto are possible, and two or three days minimum are needed to see Kyoto's splendors.

Among the "must see" spots are: the Gion area, with the Gion corner offering traditional arts and performances; the Kinkakuji (Temple of the Golden Pavilion); the Ryoanji (rock and sand garden); the old Kyoto Imperial Palace; the Nijo Shogun Palace; the University of Kyoto; Doshisha University; Daitokuji Temple; Kiyomizu Temple; Sanjusangendo; Kokedera (the Moss Temple); the Ginkakuji (Silver

Pavilion); and the Maruyama Park. Needing special permission for entry, but worth the trouble of securing passes from the government agency in charge, are the Katsura Detached Palace, actively used by the imperial household, and the Shugakuin; both are magnificent gardens with ponds, tea houses and walkways that transport the visitor into another world. The traditional arts of Kyoto — silk weaving, cloth dyeing, embroidery, porcelain and lacquerware, dolls, fans, and cloisonne — are available for purchase, and for observation. The Kyoto Handicraft Center offers a chance to watch these artifacts being made.

Kyushu

Of the four major islands of Japan, Kyushu is the third largest, and is in the southwesternmost part of the country. It connects to Honshu, the main island, by railway tunnels, a bridge, and a highway tunnel. Occupying just over 11% of the total land space of Japan, its nearly 14,000,000 inhabitants form the second most populated island of Japan. There are four national parks, many scenic sea coasts, mountains, and famous hot spring resorts. Nagasaki, the second city to be atom-bombed, is rich in history and thrives as a tourist center for both Japanese and foreigner. Two mountains, Mt. Aso in the north — the world's largest volcano — and Sakurajima, in Kagoshima, are symbols of the natural beauty of the island. Beppu, in the northeast, is a world famous spa. Historically, Kyushu is considered the bridge over which continental Asian culture passed into Japan. It also served as the gateway to Western culture for over 500 years, before and during the period when Japan closed its doors to outside influence beginning in the 17th Century.

L

Labor Unions

Some 35% of the labor force, numbering 12 million, are labor union members in Japan; this is a much higher percentage than in the U.S. Labor unions in Japan, however, behave very differently from those in the U.S. Government employees, national railroad and postal workers, as well as teachers, belong to national unions. But most employees of business and industry belong to enterprise (i.e., company) unions. Each union is made up of both blue collar and white collar workers. Most of these unions are affiliated with either Sohyo, a federation led by the Socialist Party, or Domei, a federation led by the Democratic Socialist Party.

Through the nationwide "spring offensive" (*Shunto*), an annual labor campaign for higher wages and better working conditions is mounted with vigor. Crippling and damaging work stoppages are rare, owing to the nature of enterprise unions; the welfare of the members is regarded as identical to the health of the company itself.

Days lost as a result of labor disputes are fewer than one-third of those in the U.S. It is important to note that some U.S.-Japan joint ventures (Japanese owned companies in the U.S.) do not, to date, have labor unions.

Language

There is a myth held by both Japanese and non-Japanese that the Japanese language is a difficult language to learn. The grammar is very different from that of the English language ... unlike the study of European languages, an American does not have the advantage of cognates ("constitution" in English is "constitution" in French). However, Japanese is far from being a formidable language to learn. In fact, the pronunciation is simple and the grammer is very systematic, with much fewer exceptions to the rules than in English. An increasing number of Americans are acquiring spoken language capability. What differs most from European languages — and this is the reason it takes longer to learn Japanese — is its writing system. The writing system is made up of three kinds of letter-symbols: *kanji* (often called Chinese ideographs or characters), *hiragana*, and *katakana*. *Kanji* are symbols with sounds and meaning, and function much like the symbols "%" and "$" appearing in written English sentences. The *hiragana* and *katakana* are phonetic symbols, each representing either vowel sounds or a consonant-vowel syllabic cluster (technically called a syllabary). The former is predominantly used; the latter is used to inscribe loan words from foreign languages, such as "Kurisumasu" (Japanized from "Christmas"). Though it is possible to write every Japanese word in romanization, the use is limited to auxiliary functions. Linguistically, the Japanese language is often classified as a member of the Ural-Altaic language group. It has structural resemblances to Korean and Mongolian, but striking dissimilarities to Chinese. Its origin and linguistic "family" connections have not been well established. Some scholars even claim to have discovered the origin in the Burmese highlands or in the South Pacific, but the evidence cited has not been conclusive.

Laws And Legal System
See Also: GOVERNMENT; POLITICS

The modern Japanese legal system has basically been a codified law patterned after those of continental Europe. After World War II, some elements of the Anglo-American common law system, such as broadened individual rights, have been incorporated. The 1947 Constitution stipulates a single national court network which presently is comprised of a Supreme Court (with 15 justices), eight appellate courts, fifty district courts, and other courts with limited jurisdiction (family courts, traffic courts, and small claims courts). Supreme Court justices are appointed by the prime minister, and the Supreme Court nominates lower court judges.

There is no jury system. In criminal cases, prosecutors (sometimes referred to as procurators) exercise broader discretionary power than their American counterparts; they bring charges only where there is strong evidence, and exercise much influence on criminals' rehabilitation programs. This process produces a 99% conviction rate, although punishments imposed are generally lenient.

All lawyers, judges, and prosecutors are graduates of the Legal Research and Training Institute administered by the Supreme Court. The Institute is a two-year postgraduate school which accepts only a few hundred applicants annually, based on their scores in a highly competitive examination. On a per capita basis, there are fewer than one twentieth as many lawyers in Japan than in the U.S. (There are more lawyers in the greater Chicago area than in all of Japan.) Despite this seemingly low number of lawyers, most Japanese feel that their judicial system functions adequately.

Japan is not a litigious society; most conflicts are resolved by means other than litigation. Non-litigious resolutions are possible largely owing to the homogeneity of the Japanese cultural, language and ethnic make-up. Japanese, however, are very legalistic and tend to follow the letter of the law strictly.

M

Major Sites

Tokyo Area:
Akihabara
Forty-seven ronin gravesite
Ginza
Hibiya Park
Imperial Palace
Kabuki Theater
Kanze Kaikan Noh Theatre
Meiji Shrine
Shimbashi
Shinjuku
Shinjuku Gardens
Tsukiji fish market
Tokyo Tower
Yasukuni Shrine

Near Tokyo:
Atami
Chiba Peninsula
Enoshima
Fuji
Hakone
Kamakura Buddha
Miura Peninsula
Nikko
   Kegon Falls
   Lake Chuzenji
   Nikko Shrines
Oiso Beach

Yokohama:
Gaijin Bochi
Harbor tours
Isezaki-cho
Motomachi
Sankeien
Sojiji Temple

Nagoya:
Higashiyama Zoo
Nagoya Castle
Noritake China factory

Ise:
Grand Shrines
Hydrofoil cruises
Mikimoto pearl farm

Kyoto:
Kinkakuji and Ginkakuji pavilions
Kiyomizu Temple
Moss Garden
Nijo (Shogun's) Palace
Old Imperial Palace
Ryoanji Temple and Gardens

Nara:
Deer Park
Horyuji
Pagoda
Tennoji Shrine and Buddha

Osaka:
National Bunraku Theater
Dohtombori recreation district
Osaka Castle

Gifu:
Cormorant fishing party

Hiroshima:
Atom Bomb Memorial Park
   and Museum
Miyajima Island

Inland Sea:
Cities of Okayama, Kurashiki, and Matsushima

Nagasaki:
Atomic Bomb site
Chinese quarter
"Madam Butterfly's House"
Old Christian churches

Sendai:
Matsushima National Park

Sapporo:
Ainu villages nearby
Snow Festival

Medical Insurance

For those who are not covered for medical treatment and hospitalization, and if some insurance coverage is needed, there is the International Association for Medical Assistance to Travelers, with head offices in New York City. The *Eisei Byoin* (See Appendix) is the Association's Tokyo representative institution. A directory of doctors and facilities with English language ability is included in membership. The worldwide listing shows information for Kyoto, Osaka as well as Tokyo, and a 24-hour service is offered, with general practitioners and specialists on call.

Meiji

Meiji is the name of an era in Japan (1868 to 1912) as well as the posthumous name of Emperor Mutsuhito, whose reign ushered in the restoration of imperial rule, following centuries of military domination over the throne. The Meiji ("Enlightened Rule") period witnessed vast reforms, including the promulgation of the Imperial Constitution (1889), the replacement of fiefs by prefectures, and, in general, an effective modernization plan which looked to Western technologies to complement Eastern values. Modern (meaning Western) innovations included railways (the first, between Tokyo and Yokohama, was started in 1872), communications, arts, industries and customs from America and Europe.

The Meiji Restoration witnessed the shift from an agrarian economy, where wealth was measured in terms of quantities of rice, to a town-centered currency system utilized by a flourishing merchant class. Concepts of democracy, freedom of thought, equality of educational opportunity and international recognition guided the once isolated country into the international arena. Leaders in the Meiji period included such giants as Fukuzawa Yukichi. They were responsible and selfless men whose mark is still felt on the country.

Meishi

In the Japanese business community, it is expected that business cards (*meishi*) will be exchanged at the initial introduction. Not to carry *meishi* is considered a *faux-pas* in Japanese business culture, and many Japanese businessmen will not talk to individuals who have failed to present cards. *Meishi* should be printed in both Japanese and English and should include your title or position. It is also advisable to buy a holder for your business cards. Cultural expectations aside, the bi-lingual business card offers a practical advantage in that Japanese sometimes have difficulty remembering American names.

Metric System

The metric system is used throughout Japan. Here is a selective table of weights and measures:

1 foot .... 30.48 cm	1 inch .... 2.54 cm
1 kilometer .... 0.621 mile	1 mile .... 1.609 km
1 meter .... 3.280 feet	1 meter .... 1.094 yards
1 centimeter ... 0.394 inch	1 yard .... 0.914 meter
1 pound ...... 0.454 kilogram	1 ounce ...... 28.350 grams
1 kilogram .... 2.205 pounds	1 gram .... 0.035 ounce
0 centigrade ... 32 Fahrenheit	20 centigrade... 68 Fahrenheit
30 centigrade ... 86 Fahrenheit	100 centigrade. .212 Fahrenheit

MITI

See Also: ADMINISTRATIVE GUIDANCE

The acronym for the Ministry of International Trade and Industry. This is one of the most powerful and influential of all the Japanese government agencies. It has guided post-World War II development and expansion of international trade. In Japan, the best and brightest college students seek work with the government bureaucracy, especially with MITI, the Ministry of Finance, and the Ministry of Foreign Affairs.

MITI's various bureaus gather information worldwide for their respective industries and commercial sectors. They then plan, set goals and manage objectives, with timetables, through the process known as administrative guidance. MITI perhaps has been most responsible for creating the image of "Japan, Inc." by carefully and successfully orchestrating business and industrial activities. MITI's influence is so strong that, at times, its activities abroad could overshadow those of the Foreign Ministry. There are MITI agencies in major cities of the world, known as JETRO (Japan External Trade Organization) or the Japan Trade Center.

Music And Musical Instruments

Traditional music, and the instruments on which it is performed, is, at first exposure, exotic and strange to the Western ear. Japanese have enthusiastically kept alive the nation's musical traditions, and, at the same time, have embraced Western musical forms and instrumentation. Therefore, music in Japan exists on two tracks, mostly separate, but which overlap in the music of some modern composers. The

Western musical track features orchestras, soloists, small ensembles, opera, ballet, musicals, jazz, rock and country Western, which are performed regularly by Japanese and foreign musicians. On the other hand, *hogaku* (Music of Japan) is heard on television, radio, in the movies, on the stage, and in the traditional performing arts of every variety.

Japanese music has developed uniquely on Japanese soil, although the instruments, and many other poetic and musical influences from China, survive. While Western music is both melodic and harmonic, traditional Japanese five-tone scales utilize whole, half, quarter, and even narrower steps, achieving a 20 or 30 note octave, as opposed to the twelve notes in the octave in most Western music.

Music came from China and Korea in the Nara Period (600 to 784) and was performed by foreign musicians for the Imperial Court. By the Heian Period, encompassing some four centuries, ending in 1192, Japanese innovations and performance reached maturity. The music of the court, still performed as *Gagaku*, employs instruments such as the drum, the zither-like koto, the horizontal flute, an oboe-like instrument, called the *hichiriki*, a gong and the *sho*, a "mouth organ" which produces a tone cluster.

The most popular instruments today are the *koto*, the *shakuhachi*, and the *shamisen*. The *koto* (six-feet long, wooden, with 13 strings made of silk or plastic) has become the musical instrument learned by young ladies in the home, as part of their training in the fine arts. Like the piano, most everyone has played (or played with) it. The *shakuhachi* is the bamboo flute that is popular among men, and which, like the *koto*, can be performed in solo or as part of an ensemble. A group which combines these three instruments is the *jiuta*. The third instrument of this group is the *shamisen*, long one of the most popular instruments in the entertainment world. Technically a "three-string plucked chordophone," it is somewhat similar to the banjo. The *shamisen* is used in Bunraku (*q.v.*), Kabuki (*q.v.*), and by the Geisha (*q.v.*).

N

Nagoya

Nagoya is Japan's fourth largest city with a population of approximately 2,100,000 in a 200 square mile area. Exactly two hours by Bullet Train from Tokyo, Nagoya is a well-planned commercial center with wide streets and a variety of business, shopping and sightseeing opportunities for foreigners. As the Aichi prefectural capital, it has an imposing castle built by the first shogun, Tokugawa Ieyasu, for his son Yoshinao in 1610. The castle, along with most of Nagoya, was destroyed in wartime raids. As one of the leading manufacturing cities in Japan, it has long been known for its ceramics (Noritake china company is here), with nearby Seto giving its name to the generic pottery made from the abundant supply of clay. Ninety-two percent of Japan's export of chinaware comes from Nagoya. Heavy industries have added to this image, with automobiles (Toyota City is nearby), shipbuilding, machinery, plastics, drugs and chemicals. Aside from the castle, the Tokugawa Art Museum offers items of interest to the history buff, while the separate large-scale clusters of shopping and amusement centers cater to other tastes. The Higashiyama Park has one of Japan's new zoos, where no fences obstruct the view of the animals.

Names

When speaking and writing in Japanese, the family name is mentioned before the given name. Japanese as a rule do not have middle names. The most common way the Japanese address one another is by the family name, plus "san," a suffix meaning Mr./Mrs./Miss/Ms. Below are other suffixes used and their social significance:

Family name plus "*sensei*": Any person in the teaching profession, from a nursery school teacher to a college professor; a tutor in a tea ceremony or an abacus instructor; all are referred to in this way, or simply called "*sensei*." Medical doctors and politicians are also addressed in this manner, as well as, occasionally, the most senior person within an organization.

Given name plus "chan": Diminutive usage; used only among children or young lovers.

Family name plus "kun": Male use only, between colleagues of equal rank and classmates; seniors will address a junior, or younger male colleague, with this term.

Unlike in American society, where there is pressure to get on a first-name basis as soon as possible as an indication that there is no pretention about one's status, there is no equivalent tendency in Japan. For a Japanese to call another Japanese by the first name is a totally unexpected, and even alarming, event. But Japanese have come to expect foreigners to use their first names, although it definitely cuts against the grain, and should be avoided.

In still other cases, the surname may be avoided when addressing a company president or official of high rank. One calls him by the title he bears, such as *shacho san* (Mr. President); *bucho san* (Department Chief); *gakucho san* (College President); etc.

Generally, the first name of most Japanese clues one to the gender of the person. Female first names very often end in "ko." They may also end in "e." Male first names end in "o" or "ro." (See appendix.)

Nara

Nara is the center stage of early Japanese history. It is located about an hour by train from either Kyoto or Osaka, and about four hours from Tokyo. The capital of Nara Prefecture, it is populated by about a quarter of a million people. It is one of the great historical repositories in Japan. In 710 A.D. Nara was made the first permanent capital of the country, and the eight imperial reigns from that time give the period up to 784 the name, "Late Nara Period." The artifacts, such as jewels, glassware, musical instruments, silver, writing materials, apparel, and all manner of precious objects, are contained in the securely sealed *Shosoin*, the Treasure Repository of the Imperial Household. Other important cultural and architectural treasures are in the *Todaiji* (Great Eastern Temple), which contains one of the largest bronze statues of Buddha in the world and is designated "national treasure." Temples abound, and the setting for them is idyllic: the Sarusawa Pond, and the Deer Park (where the deer roam freely and feed on hand-held biscuits, much to the delight of children). The Nara National Museum, dating from 1895, is near the Deer Park.

National Holidays
See Also: FESTIVALS
There are twelve days during the year which are observed by government and public offices, banks, post offices, schools, etc. as holidays. In chronological order, they are:

JANUARY 1.   New Year's Day (*Ganjitsu*). The beginning of the new year is celebrated as Japan's most important holiday. It is a time when "business as usual" ceases for several days.

JANUARY 15.

Adult's Day (*Seijin no hi*). On this day, youth who have reached the age of 20 are honored and accepted as adults by society.

FEBRUARY 11.

National Foundation Day (*Kenkoku Kinembi*). According to tradition, Jimmu became the country's first Emperor on this day in the year ca. 600 B.C.

MARCH 20 OR 21.

Vernal Equinox Day (*Shumbun no hi*). The first day of spring when the goodness of nature is celebrated.

APRIL 29.

Emperor's Birthday (*Tenno tanjobi*). On his birthday, Emperor Hirohito customarily appears on the balcony of the Tokyo Imperial Palace to greet the public who are rarely admitted to the grounds.

MAY 3.

Constitution Day (*Kempo kinembi*). Anniversary of the enforcement of the post-War Constitution.

MAY 5.

Children's Day (*Kodomo no hi*). Both boys and girls are honored by the nation. Before the War, this day was reserved for Boys' Day; Girls' Day was formerly celebrated on March 3.

SEPTEMBER 15.

Day of Respect for the Elderly (*Keiro no hi*).

SEPTEMBER 23 OR 24.

Autumnal Equinox Day (*Shubun no hi*). Ancestors are worshipped on this occasion.

OCTOBER 10.

Sports Day (*Taiiku no hi*). Sports as a means of maintaining physical and mental health are celebrated.

NOVEMBER 3.

Culture Day (*Bunka no hi*). A day when those who have contributed to the cultural well-being of the country are honored by the government with awards for artistic and literary accomplishments.

NOVEMBER 23.

Labor Thanksgiving Day (*Kinro Kansha no hi*). The nation honors its workers.

61

Natural Resources

The most abundant natural resource in Japan is water. Sulfur and clay are also plentiful. Rice is produced sufficiently within the country. But there is either a deficiency or a total absence of all other raw materials required to sustain life and provide the basic ingredients for subsistance and industry. (The U.S. imports some 20% of its raw material needs.) Following is a list of the major resources imported by Japan, listed in order of decreasing dependence:

All energy sources	87%	Copper	95.6%
Aluminum	100%	Soybeans	95.4%
Corn	100%	Wheat	93.0%
Cotton	100%	Natural Gas	88.7%
Nickel	100%	Lead	82.4%
Wool	100%	Coal	79.2%
Oil	99.8%	Lumber	69.2%
Iron Ore	98.6%	Zinc	68.7%
Tin	97.7%		

Japan is the world's largest importer of oil, coal and iron ore, cotton, wool and lumber. With these raw material imports, Japan creates value-added manufactured goods for home consumption and export. The exports pay for the cost of the raw materials. Leading export items include autos and auto parts, steel mill products, trucks, business machines, audio/stereo equipment, and motorcycles and parts.

New Year

On January 1, the Emperor observes the ancient rite of praying for bountiful crops and the nation's prosperity. Shrines nationwide participate in similar solemnities. This sets the tone for the most important and extensive holiday in Japan. In the latter part of December, decorations (*kadomatsu*) are placed in the home and public places to usher in the new year, which usually precedes the Chinese new year but takes the name of the animal of the next Chinese year. Year-end cards are sent, and although they are not as fancy as Christmas cards, bear the sign of the new year animal and carry a new year's message. The cards are mailed early enough to guarantee delivery on *Ganjitsu*, the "first day." Special foods, not ordinarily eaten during the year, are prepared for the ceremonial New Year's meal. The foods chosen are symbolic of good luck and are important for the significance and sound of their names, rather than just the taste.

Newspapers

Japan is a universally literate society, and the printed word has enjoyed a high status in transmitting information. Newspapers continue to play a key role as Japan moves beyond industrialization into the production of services which depends so much on informed people. As one of the world's most successful enterprises, Japan's newspaper industry contains over 100 dailies, most of which are published in several editions. Over 50 million copies a day are sold, and circulation figures compete well with the U.S. and U.S.S.R. Japan is first worldwide in per capita circulation. The top five dailies are published both in Tokyo and Osaka. They are: *Asahi, Mainichi, Yomiuri, Sankei,* and *Nihon Keizai. Asahi, Mainichi,* and *Yomiuri* have English language dailies, which are available in major hotels, train stations and airports, and bookstores in the larger cities.

Nikko

One of the most popular of the 27 national parks in Japan, Nikko ("light of the sun") is a grand memorial and mausolea complex encompassing the tombs of Tokugawa Ieyasu (1542-1616) and his grandson Iemitsu. In addition to the magnificent edifices, there are natural surroundings which make the trip to Nikko a memorable experience, and which can be accomplished in one day. It is conveniently reached by train from Asakusa (Tokyo). Taking one hour and forty-five minutes on the "Romance Car" of the Tobu Line, the trip is made in comfort and convenience. Other sites include Lake Chuzenji, with its shops and recreational facilities, the Kegon Falls, Japan's most famous waterfall, and the *Irohazaka,* a winding road between the mausolea and the lake which offers spectacular views with each new turn in the road. A popular saying in Japanese sums it up: "Never say *kekko* (splendid) until you've seen Nikko."

Noh

Sometimes described as "moving sculpture," the stately stage art of the *Noh* is indeed an understated dance form which seeks to unify the allied arts of music and acting in a manner at once solemn and beautiful. "*Noh*" is a Buddhist term which alludes to the mental bond between the performers and the audience. Over 100 years old, it progressed from very humble beginnings (in the dances of peasants) to become, in the 14th Century, the major entertainment of the court nobility and associated aristocracy. It continues today to appeal to those who relive the past through the libretti of such famous *Noh* plays as Takasago, Funabenkei, and Basho. The chief performers wear masks, which add to the low-keyed dramatic gestures for which *Noh* has long been revered. Serenity, seriousness, and tragedy are much the mood of *Noh.* Interludes of comedy relief (*kyogen,* or "mad words" they are called) are needed to provide a proper balance to the pathos of the plays, which last hours on end.

Okinawa

Formerly known as the Ryukyu Island Group, Okinawa is now a prefecture under the control of the Japanese government. It became such under the terms of the 1972 agreement with the U.S. to return the some 60 islands (four island groups) occupied by America after World War II. Okinawa lies 425 miles off the southern tip of Kyushu and has a population of just over one million. By air it is 2.5 hours from Tokyo. Having a subtropical climate, Okinawa owes much of its unique cultural makeup to the influences of China and Southeast Asia. Naha is the prefectural capital. The economy is agriculturally-based with fishing and livestock, sugar, and pineapples, and their processed derivatives, the major industries. A souvenir specialty of Okinawa is the colorful *Bingata*, a cotton/silk/linen fabric used in clothing and decorations for the home.

Omoiyari And Enryo

Anticipating another's needs rather than acting upon a specific request, *omoiyari* is considered a preferred and virtuous way in Japan. Thus the Japanese may serve drinks without asking what their guests would like, or may call a taxi for a departing business client before one is asked for. Such behavior is appreciated by Japanese and is called *omoiyari*, literally meaning "consideration." Holding back one's request, or hesitating to put forth one's needs for fear of imposing on others, is called *"enryo,"* literally meaning "distant consideration." The Japanese practice a great deal of *enryo* in the company of strangers since there is no established relationship (See *Amae*). Neither *omoiyari* nor *enryo* is an alien concept in the West, but the Japanese tend to carry such behavior to a much greater degree.

On And Giri

A highly defined and somewhat ritualized sense of personal obligation exists in Japan. This finds its roots in the related concepts of *on* and *giri*. *On* is a sense of indebtedness towards one's superiors (including an organization to which one belongs). The obligation comes from a favor or assistance provided in times of need. One is bound to try to repay the good deed, by being loyal, for the rest of one's life, and does so with determination to serve the superior or the organization. The assumption is, however, that the debt may never be fully repaid. The prototype of *on* is found in a child's obligation to parents for their care and concern in the rearing process.

Giri is also an obligation to act in an expected manner toward other members of society, but in whom there is no incurred indebtedness. *Giri* principles apply to one's associates, and behavior depends upon the relative societal position. Gift-giving (*q.v.*) embraces some of these principles: one may give because of the protocols demanding a gift, not because of a will to give *per se*. The "*giri* relationship" is reciprocal, since, in return for a demonstration of loyalty on the part of an inferior (such as through gift-giving), the superior is obligated to show responsibility and a caring attitude.

Opera

For the most part, opera in Japan is Western opera, usually sung in the original language, but, when performed by some local troupes, may be translated into Japanese. Some pre- and post-War composers have created operas on the Western model. Dan Ikuma's "Yuzuru" is a specific example of Japanese mythology put to operatic purposes and organized very much like a Western opera. The Japanese are enthusiastic supporters of both visiting and resident opera companies which tour the country regularly and receive special attention. In Tokyo it is not unusual to count over one hundred opera performances in one year. The first opera performed in Japan was Gluck's "Orpheus," in 1903. Thirty years later the first Japanese troupe, the Fujiwara Opera Company, was formed, and is the primary company today; it mounts productions regularly. Other substantial companies include the Nagato Opera Company, the Niki-Kai, and the Tokyo Chamber Opera Company. The English language newspapers carry announcements about opera performances which are held in several magnificent halls capable of handling the staging requirements of opera.

Origami

Origami is "folded paper." Folding paper, however, comprises components of the decorative arts, the challenges of a game, and the frivolity of a pastime; it is most popular among young girls. The art aspect is evident in the skills required and the beauty of the final product — a multi-folded paper of one or more colors which forms a crane, a boat or a flower, to name just a few of the thousands of possible shapes *origami* might take. Paper sizes vary from about six inches square, to under one inch square — which show off the manual dexterity of anyone with sufficient patience and eyesight. *Origami* probably pre-dates the 17th Century, when it became very popular. It remains so, and competes well with modern toys and television for the attention of the young and old.

Osaka

Osaka is the major urban center of West Central Honshu. As such, it forms the heart of the Kansai (or Kinki) district of Japan. The district is integrated along an urban corridor occupied by Kyoto, Osaka, and Kobe. With a population in excess of three million, Osaka is the seat of Osaka Prefecture. It shares control over the national economy of Japan with its arch rival, Tokyo. Osaka is the traditional business center of Japan; major commercial enterprises started here in early modern times. The city lies on the delta formed by the flow of the Yodo River into Osaka Bay. There are 26 wards which subdivide the city into geopolitical units. By Bullet Train, it is just three hours and ten minutes from Tokyo, and 12 minutes from Kyoto. The Itami International Airport is within an hour's train ride, and the flight to Tokyo is fifty-five minutes.

As to sights, Osaka boasts the famous feudal castle built in 1586 by Toyotomi Hideyoshi, a remarkable military leader. The Osaka Castle was the scene of a fierce battle in 1615 between the Tokugawa and Toyotomi clans. The present structure is a concrete replica and serves as a museum. Dohtombori is a popular amusement quarter along a canal. In the evening the neon lights glisten off the canal, and the restaurants and night spots do a good business. In the same area, the famous puppet shows (*bunraku*) (*q.v.*) are performed at the National Puppet Theater. The Tennoji Temple nearby was founded by the most venerable historical figure of Japan, Prince Shotoku, in 593. The temple predates the Horyuji Temple in Nara, Japan's oldest wooden structure.

P

Pharmacies

There are many drug stores in Japan, but few of them have the items familiar to foreigners. In major hotels, most medicines needed for minor ailments can be purchased from English-speaking staff. In Tokyo, a comprehensive supply of imported pharmaceutical goods is available at the American Pharmacy in Yurakucho (See appendix). Prescriptions can be filled there or at hospitals and clinics with which the prescribing physician is affiliated.

Police

See Also: CRIME

Some 185,000 policemen are on duty in Japan, and can be located readily by phone in emergencies, or at one of two places: in a *koban*, a square hut with the police emblem over the door (and often a red light as well); or, on the corner in urban centers. Patrol cars are used in sparsely populated areas and on highways, but the patrolman on foot is more common. There are over 6000 *koban* in Japan. These huts date from the early Edo days, when stations were set up at intersections to control violence, or *tsujigiri* (street corner murders).

Being a policeman in Japan today is not considered a dangerous job. Unlike pre-War times, the people trust the police and go to them readily when they, or their family, are in trouble, or they suspect criminal activity. In America, by contrast, someone in trouble may first seek legal counsel. Japanese are encouraged to go to the *koban*, or call a nationally known number. There are no jurisdictional problems, and police can handle a case anywhere and receive the cooperation of police elsewhere in the country. When a crime is reported, the police are swift to move into an investigation, and have a high rate of arrests — close to 70% of all crimes end in convictions in Japan, as opposed to 20% average in America. The more serious crimes, like murder, have a 96% rate of arrest and conviction.

Politics

See Also: LAWS AND LEGAL SYSTEM; GOVERNMENT

Since 1945, Japan has been a "democratic" country, with a form of government similar to that of the British structure: the Emperor presides over a constitutional monarchy as a symbol of the unity of the people. The 1947 Constitution calls for a political framework based on the U.S. model. The Constitution guarantees basic human rights, such as the freedom of expression and assembly. With political parties, voters, campaigns, national and local representatives, a bicameral legislature, courts of law, government ministries, and political scandals, it is tempting to interpret the scene in Western political terms. "Democracy" in Japan is not "majority rule" but "action by concensus." Political parties, therefore, exist to represent divergent views, which somehow must all be incorporated into national goals and policies, however minor the party.

The continuous post-War ruling political group has been the Liberal Democratic Party (LDP), and its direct predecessors under different names. This leadership has offered the country political continuity and stability since 1945. The LDP comprises several strong factions, the strongest of which in any given election controls the legislature, the National Diet. The strong men of the dominant faction agree upon whom they will promote as the Prime Minister, who is then formally elected to the post by the House of Representatives. The Prime Minister's Cabinet of 20 ministers and heads of government agencies perform as the executive body of the government. Other major political parties in Japan are the Japan Socialist Party, Japan Communist Party, Clean Government Party (*Komeito*), and the Democratic Socialist Party. There are currently a total of 491 seats in the House of Representatives and 252 members of the House of Councillors.

Population
See Also: RACIAL MIXTURE
Japan's population in 1986 was about 121,490,000 (roughly one-half the 241,600,000 in the U.S.). About 10% of the population are located in Tokyo, and the percentage is greater when the more than 20,000,000 residents of greater Tokyo, including Yokohama, are counted. Three-quarters of the entire population live between Tokyo and Kobe, and include large concentrations in the major cities of Nagoya, Kyoto, and Osaka (*q.v.*) in between. This population belt is known as the "*Tokaido*," or Eastern Seaboard. Growth in the birthrate is held to less than 1% per year, yet the population grows one million annually. Longevity, which is currently at age 81 for women and 75 for men, adds to the growing numbers. Population density is 815 people per square mile (compared with 63 per square mile in the U.S.).

Prefectures
In 1947 the Diet passed the Local Autonomy Law, which provided a system in principle close to "home rule," modified by a set of rules for the uniform structure and activities of the various types of local governmental bodies. Prefectures were among the political entities affected by this legislation. Although prefectures are designed to serve as intermediary bodies between the cities, towns, villages, and the state, these pivotal links in the national pattern of political and geographical control have continued to the present in a controversial

role amidst the struggle of national recentralization versus the maintenance of pure local autonomy. Their position in the geopolitical sense is not comparable to states in the U.S., but is similar to English counties.

The forty-seven prefectures in Japan are referred to by four different designations, *to, do, fu,* or *ken,* according to their administrative structure or the characteristics of their jurisdiction. There is one *to*: Tokyo, one *do*: Hokkaido, two *fu*: Kyoto and Osaka, and forty-three *ken.* Tokyo-*to* differs from other prefectures in that is has 23 special wards (*ku*). Following is a list of each prefecture in Japan, and its capital city:

Aichi	Nagoya	Miyazaki	Miyazaki
Akita	Akita	Nagano	Nagano
Aomori	Aomori	Nagasaki	Nagasaki
Chiba	Chiba	Nara	Nara
Ehime	Matsuyama	Niigata	Niigata
Fukui	Fukui	Oita	Oita
Fukuoka	Fukuoka	Okayama	Okayama
Fukushima	Fukushima	Okinawa	Naha
Gifu	Gifu	Osaka	Osaka
Gumma	Maebashi	Saga	Saga
Hiroshima	Hiroshima	Saitama	Urawa
Hokkaido	Sapporo	Shiga	Otsu
Hyogo	Kobe	Shimane	Matsue
Ibaraki	Mito	Shizuoka	Shizuoka
Ishikawa	Kanazawa	Tochigi	Utsunomiya
Iwate	Morioka	Tokushima	Tokushima
Kagawa	Takamatsu	Tokyo	Tokyo
Kagoshima	Kagoshima	Tottori	Tottori
Kanagawa	Yokohama	Toyama	Toyama
Kochi	Kochi	Wakayama	Wakayama
Kumamoto	Kumamoto	Yamagata	Yamagata
Kyoto	Kyoto	Yamaguchi	Yamaguchi
Mie	Tsu	Yamanashi	Kofu
Miyagi	Sendai		

Privacy

In the group-oriented traditional Japanese society (See Groups), the concept of privacy as the Western world knows it is considered neither important nor beneficial. In fact, when the Western legal system was introduced during the Meiji era (*q.v.*) the term *shiken* ("private rights") had to be newly coined.

Though modern Japanese do respect a certain Western sense of privacy and laws protecting the privacy of an individual, some traditional sentiments of holding collective interests over and above individual rights are likely to remain for a long time to come. Senior members in a Japanese company, for example, tend to know far more about the private lives of their subordinates than their American counterparts would. In fact, they often feel that they have a right to know, as such information is relevant to the company's well being.

R

Racial Mixture
See Also: BURAKUMIN

Japan is racially, linguistically, and culturally one of the most homogeneous countries in the world. The minority population, making up much less than one percent of the entire population, includes about 600,000 Koreans (brought to Japan during World War II to supplement the labor force), a few tens of thousands of Chinese, and fewer than 20,000 Ainu (*q.v.*). The Ainu are found only in Hokkaido today, though their ancestors lived as far south as present day Tokyo until the 8th Century.

Japan has been relatively free of ethnic problems, with the exception of Koreans and *burakumin* (*q.v.*) who are racially Japanese, but have been discriminated against as social outcast groups.

Religions
See Also: FESTIVALS; DATING AND MARRIAGE; FUNERALS

The spiritual life of the Japanese derives from the various beliefs and faiths held by the people. First among these beliefs are the myths that explain the national origin. The concept that the country is of "divine origin" is one of the original beliefs that still shapes individual and organizational attitudes. *Shinto* (literally, the Way of the Gods) is the indigenous religion stemming from nature worship. It embodies rites and rituals both primitive in character and revered as the emotional basis of Japanese religious faith. Because it is the ethnic, or original, religion, all others, such as Buddhism, Christianity, and Judaism, are viewed as imported or borrowed. Generally speaking, the imported religions have been treated equally and fairly throughout history, with some exceptions.

In fact, it has become impossible to separate pure Shintoism from pure Buddhism, as the parallel existence of the two for centuries has caused a blending, and hence a blurring of distinctions between them. Introduced in the 6th Century A.D. from Korea, Buddhism has greatly influenced Japanese cultural life and social order, adding much to the arts, government, education, literature, language, and behavior of the people. While the essential symbolism and certain features of the two religions are distinct, and their respective roles somewhat defined, the Japanese have felt that relating to each of them has provided a greater understanding of their special characteristics.

Each have proscribed domains, and offer religious activity that is complementary, quite to the liking of the Japanese. They have not tended, as a people, to be exclusivist about sectarian religion.

Christianity, associated with Western culture and spirituality, was introduced in the 16th Century by Francis Xavier, a Spanish Jesuit. Like Buddhism, Christianity was first welcomed, then persecuted and rejected for a period of time. Both religions are evangelistic in nature, and have developed a variety of competing sects. Unlike Buddhism, Christianity has remained relatively small in numbers (some 2% of the population), although its political and educational influence far exceed the implications of size. The 1947 Constitution guarantees religious freedom in Japan. When asked, many Japanese respond that they are not members of a specific religious order, yet all are actively involved in some programs fostered by shrines, temples, and churches. In large cities, most religious denominations, including Jewish, Moslem, and others, provide worship services for foreign visitors. A list of services appears in English language newspapers.

Restaurants

Because restaurants of every size and specialty exist throughout Japan, it is impossible to single out the best. As a rule, major hotels serve excellent Western food and have a number of facilities offering a variety of Japanese foods. A list of Tokyo restaurants especially attractive to foreigners, both for the food and the setting, can be found in the appendix.

These first-class eateries have a lot of competition. Even the small specialty food shops seating only 25 to 30 offer good food at reasonable prices. Department stores have good food as well; in common with all of the inexpensive spots are the plastic models displayed in the windows. Selections can be pointed to if language is a problem. Invariably, what you get is very much like what you see displayed, and is tasty. Prices in the cheaper places are from ¥500 to ¥1500; prices can soar in excess of ¥10,000 a person at the most expensive restaurants, including those in major hotels. Lunches are about 20% cheaper, and Western-style breakfasts are impossible to find outside of hotels.

Ringi And Nemawashi
See Also: COMPANY STRUCTURE

Ringi ("circulating documents") and *nemawashi* ("attending to roots," or "touching all bases") are part and parcel of Japanese business decision-making processes. *Ringi* is a means whereby management decisions are arrived at by circulating written proposals (*ringi-sho*) prepared by lower-level management. As proposals circulate, a large number of persons affix their seal (*q.v.*) indicating their agreement, or the fact that they have seen the documents and do not oppose their contents. The person originating the *ringi-sho* makes sure the proposal will be accepted by conducting many informal discussions, called *nemawashi*. *Ringi* and *nemawashi* thus are the formal and informal sides of the same consensus-based decision-making process. Arriving at a final decision takes more time than the "top-to-bottom," dictatorial style of business leadership in the U.S. But once a decision is made, implementation tends to be swift and comprehensive.

Romanization

Since the late 19th Century there have been a number of attempts to abolish the Japanese writing system, based on Chinese characters, in favor of a romanized form of writing. The last serious attempt occurred in 1946 when the U.S. Education Mission favored the establishment of a simpler system of writing based on Western language models. The impact was felt: street signs, brand names, station names, etc. are rendered in romanized form as well as in the script. But most Japanese have resisted this loss of tradition, and of a means of communicating that they are emotionally committed to. To those who complain that written Japanese is cumbersome, the Japanese argue that English spelling is inconsistent and also in need of reform. Romanization schemes have appeared in three basic forms: Hepburn, Nippon-shiki, and Kunrei-shiki. Americans respond best to the Hepburn system, devised by an Englishman. The cabinet-decreed Kunrei-shiki is used by the government, and the Nippon scheme is, for the most part, an overlap with the other two. In the language section of this book, the Hepburn system of romanization is used, with alternative spellings shown in the table of Japanese sounds at the beginning of the section.

S

Sapporo

The center of Hokkaido's political, economic, and educational activity. The seventh largest city in Japan, with a population exceeding one million, Sapporo gets its name from an Ainu (*q.v.*) word meaning "long dry river." The city is strikingly similar to American city design, with streets intersecting each other at right angles. The development of Sapporo is a recent event, having been done in 1869 by Americans under contract with the Japan Commission of Colonization.

Air and rail service from Tokyo is available, and the one hour twenty-five minute flight compares favorably to the many hours by train, owing to the transfer at Aomori onto the ferry, which adds considerably to the trip. For those not in a hurry, the train provides a variety of scenic views as the journey progresses through less populated areas of Japan.

The snow festival, held annually from February 1 to 5, is the spectacular winter ice show of delicately carved snow sculptures. Other sites include the 1972 Winter Olympic village, with active winter sports available for five or six months of the year; the University of Hokkaido; the Ainu Museum, and a host of shopping facilities, some underground; and, nearly no end to scenic mountain and seaside resorts and sightseeing spots.

Seal

In place of written signatures, the Japanese affix one's seal (called *han* or *hanko*) when signing official documents. The seal is carved on one end of an elongated piece of hardwood or ivory. When used, it is stamped in bright orange-colored ink. The seal can be used by a person other than its owner and gives the user, in effect, "power of attorney." While written signatures are now used in international transactions in Japan, use of *hanko* is still the rule within the Japanese companies and government agencies.

Sex Roles

Without a doubt, Japan is the most male chauvinistic country among the industrialized nations. Though the Constitution guarantees full legal equality of the sexes in social and economic terms, there is great discrimination against women. Increasing numbers of women enter the labor market but most quit when they marry or when the first child is born. Only a few return to the work force after their children are grown. The permanent employment or seniority system (See Company Structure) applies mainly to men.

The double moral standard, which has increasingly diminished in the U.S., remains strong in Japan. Men enjoy extensive social life outside the family, and some even engage in extra-marital sexual affairs with impunity. Married women's lives, on the other hand, revolve around their families, a few girlfriends from school days, the neighborhood, and P.T.A. activities.

In Japan's not-so-distant feudal past, samurai (who were, of course, men) were supreme. Confucianism taught women to be totally obedient to men. This philosophy was vigorously extolled until the end of World War II. Thus, Japan has a long way to go before the equality of the sexes is attained in all socio-economic relations. Most Japanese feel that a rapid change has been occurring since World War II, and, on the whole, in a positive direction. But the stereotyped sex roles have not yet been strongly challenged.

Shikoku

The smallest of Japan's four principal islands, Shikoku gets its name (meaning "four prefectures") from its major provinces: Tokushima, Kagawa, Ehime, and Kochi. Two hours and ten minutes by air from Tokyo, the island has many attractions for visitors from all parts of Japan, as well as from abroad. For the Japanese, the pilgrimage has been a custom dating from the Edo period (1603). Some 88 temples throughout the island are visited by the devout, who walk for two months to make the homage to Kobo Daishi, the Buddhist priest Kukai, in a complete and carefully planned circuit, although recently some parts of the pilgrimage are made by bus. The natural sites also attract visitors. The voyage by sea across the Inland Sea National Park (Setonaikai) is available from several ports between Osaka and Kyushu; the trip from Okayama or Hiroshima offers a view of exquisite islands dotting the horizon. In Tokushima, the *Awa Odori* folk dance is performed in annual festivals, lasting three days beginning August 15. Takamatsu has one of Japan's most manicured parks, Ritsurin. Kochi has its castle and dog fights, and Matsuyama is known for the Dogo Hot Spring.

Shinjuku

In the northwest section of Tokyo, this bustling center gets its name from its historical role as an overnight rest stop in the long journey along the Tokaido between Tokyo and Osaka. It was one of the 53 stations, or checkpoints, established by the government in early modern times. The railway station at Shinjuku handles the largest number of daily train passengers in Japan. Highrise office buildings and a thriving night life are contrasts adding to the reputation of this fast-paced and growing gateway to the greenbelt area surrounding Tokyo.

Some of the highlights of the Shinjuku area:

Botanical Gardens	Meiji Memorial Gallery
Imperial Cemetary	Meiji Shrine
Isetan Department Store	National Stadium
Keio University Hospital	Tokyo Cathedral
Kosei Nenkin Hall	Waseda University

Shogun

For many centuries up to 1868, Japan was governed by a "Shogun," who formally recognized the emperor as the ruler of Japan. However, as chief military commander and civil authority, the shogun reduced the emperor to a mere symbol. Some of the more famous shoguns were Yoritomo (1192-1199), Takauji (1338-1358), Yoshimitsu (1367-1395), Yoshimasa (1449-1474), Ieyasu (1603-1605), Iemitsu (1623-1651), and Yoshimune (1716-1745). From Ieyasu's time, the seat of the shogunate was in Edo (Tokyo).

Shopping

One of the attractions of visiting Japan is the variety of shopping available. Traditional wares, modern electrical appliances, and curios top the list of attractions. Tax-free shopping makes for an incentive difficult to ignore, and places to part with one's money abound. Airports, hotel arcades, railway station shops, the Ginza — all are there for tax-free shopping and prices are fixed. No bargaining is necessary or expected. With passport in hand, visitors are guaranteed tax-free purchases, and the Government's copy of the transaction is placed in the passport to be pulled on departure. Tax-free benefits range from 10 to 20% of retail (sometimes production) price. As a rule, items costing over ¥28,000 will be reduced by 13%. For items costing above ¥37,500, the percentage will increase. Whatever is purchased, it will usually be wrapped and probably placed in a fancy bag, not just a brown paper sack. Many guides to shopping are to be found in the hotels and one-stop shopping arcades. Popular items continue to be cameras, cloisonne and damascene, stamps and coins, kimonos, silk products, ivory, watches, pearls and other jewelry, precious metals, fur products, and all manner of electronic gadgets: radios, tape recorders, compact disks (hardware and software), slide projectors, and TV sets, to name a few. Traditional items include china and pottery, lacquer ware, *washi* (Japanese paper), wood block prints, silk screens, and antiques and folk craft items. Many of these items can be purchased in department stores listed by area in the appendix.

Shopping Arcades

Arcades offer one-stop shopping of great convenience to foreigners who speak little or no Japanese, as well as those who want to concentrate on purchases that are popular with tourists. Although all of the major hotels have concentrations of shops, the arcades are more comprehensive. Both allow for tax-free purchases. In Tokyo, the oldest is the International Arcade, located between Hibiya Park and the Ginza, situated directly under the elevated railway (Yamate Line). It stretches for several blocks, and can be entered or exited at various points along the way. Other arcades can be found in the appendix.

In Kyoto, the Handicraft Center, near the Heian Shrine, is a single highrise building with specialties according to each floor. Demonstrations of handicrafts are made daily. Handicrafts represented are: doll making, silk weaving, porcelain painting, wood block printing, jewelry and handbags.

Society

See Also: RACIAL MIXTURE; VERTICAL SOCIETY

Homogeneous race and culture. Hard working. Group-oriented. Disciplined. Strong family system. Polite. Vertical human relationships. These are some of the terms often used to describe the societal organization and behavior of the Japanese. Key among these concepts is the value placed on human relationships. An overcrowded country has learned to get along, with dense population packed into about 20% of the land area, by defining relationships clearly. To whom and to what people relate has developed from the rural setting, where growing rice requires an organized and cooperative form of human labor, and has been carried into the urban environment. The farm provided the atmosphere for a set of rankings within the family and within the society.

A sense of "place" co-exists with the rank order of people and social organizations, so that today there is strong identity with one's own or inside group, as opposed to others, or outsiders. This dichotomy begins in the family and extends to the place of work. The primary responsibility is first to one's duty or obligations defined by formal ties, work responsibilities, and national identity. Japanese do not face unknown social situations easily. There is a quiet calculation made about the "rank" or "place" of an unknown person, company or group. Until someone (or something) relates clearly to one's inner or outer circles, that person (or group) is ignored or not recognized as existing.

A relationship is neutral until known. This can be read as negative or hostile by those unfamiliar with Japan. This analysis paints a sometimes grim picture of a colorless and austere Japanese social interaction. For that reason, awkward situations are avoided and information is vital before face-to-face introductions are made. Even when relationships are clear, there is still a hierarchical environment which controls behavior. Tensions, not easily released at work or at home, are often directed to such outlets as bars, cabarets, and other night spots offering escape and diversion, especially for men.

Yet, there is an acknowledged comfort that Japanese feel in their tightly woven society. One can presume upon others, according to commonly accepted guidelines, which offers job security, marriages that continue (not necessarily happily), children that are dutiful to parents, and the elderly who are cared for and honored. Despite the outward signs of modern development and physical changes, Japan's societal inner workings are traceable to the earliest national values and institutions fostered by a large and inter-dependent population.

Sports

Both traditional and imported sports are played in Japan. The chief spectator sports are baseball and *sumo (q.v.)*. In addition to the martial arts, the highly disciplined sport of *budo (q.v.)*, the Japanese enjoy soccer, volleyball, swimming, tennis, badminton, bowling, squash, horse and car racing, roller and ice skating, basketball, gymnastics and wrestling. Japanese compete effectively in Olympic games.

By far the most popular participation sport is golf. Like tennis, however, it is a status sport and very costly. Foreigners find the green fees prohibitively expensive. Even public courses are more expensive than in the States. There are many good courses and the golf enthusiast can get information from the Japan Golf Association, in central Tokyo (Palace Bldg.).

Suicide

Japan has no religious restrictions against suicide. From feudal times, suicide has been regarded as an honorable way out of humiliation or hopelessness. Perhaps because of the conspicuous cases of kamikaze suicide missions of World War II, or the deaths of several well-known literary figures (including Yukio Mishima who committed *seppuku*), Japan has created an image of a suicide-laden society. In fact, the suicide rate in per capita terms is no more than those of other advanced nations. What troubles the Japanese is the fact that the majority of people who commit suicide are 15 to 25 years old. It is probably a reflection on the educational and employment systems which create tremendous pressure (See Education).

Seppuku, probably referred to in the West by its more vulgar term, *harakiri* ("belly cutting"), was a ritual death committed only by samurai, as a sort of "privilege" to maintain honor in the face of captivity, or humiliation from having failed to serve a master properly. It is a painful death by disembowelment, by no means a prevalent form of suicide in Japan, past or present.

Sumo

Japan's oldest sport is wrestling, called "Sumo." The matches were first held in the court of nobility or at the shrines as offerings to the gods to assure a good harvest and to promote the people's welfare. Most of what one sees in the sumo wrestling of today are ritualistic carry-overs of this ancient tradition. But most of the sacred nature of the sport has given way to a sort of cult worship of Japan's largest men, weighing in at 250 to 300 pounds. The object of the match is to cause the opponent to either lose his balance, thereby letting a part of his body touch the ground, or causing him to fall out of the ring. The Japanese Sumo Association holds six tournaments a year, each lasting fifteen days. Tokyo hosts three, and Nagoya, Osaka, and Fukuoka each host one. With an elaborate system of ranking, sumo wrestlers are upgraded or downgraded according to the number of victories in each of these tournaments.

Symphony Orchestras

The first symphony orchestra was formed in 1915, and was known as the Tokyo Philharmonic. It performed the first public concert in the same year before disbanding. Japan's finest orchestra is the NHK Symphony Orchestra, which takes its name from the Nihon Hoso Kyokai, or public broadcasting station. It was formed in 1927 by the same conductor of the defunct Philharmonic, K. Yamada. The orchestra has continued to this day.

Seven other symphony orchestras in Tokyo have been formed and attest to the popularity of Western music, and Japanese music composed for this medium. The Tokyo Symphony Orchestra, Japan Philharmonic Symphony Orchestra, Tokyo Philharmonic Orchestra, Tokyo Metropolitan Symphony Orchestra, Yomiuri Nippon Symphony Orchestra all have subscription concerts and travel around the country. Orchestras also thrive in Osaka, Kyoto, and other metropolitan areas interested in establishing for themselves names in the musical arena. In addition to the standard classical repertory of the West, Japanese composers whose music is regularly performed include Takemitsu Toru, Mayuzumi Toshiro, Akutagawa Yasushi, Akira Miyoshi, and Dan Ikuma. Both traditional and contemporary styles are represented in the concerts held in the many magnificent halls in the larger cities in Japan.

T

Table Manners

Although there are tradition-bound and elaborate customs in the Japanese polite society concerning eating and serving, there are only a few basic principles to follow. The first is that one watches and anticipates the other's needs (See *Omoiyari*). For example, one should always pour into the others' glasses, but never into one's own. Secondly, sounds such as slurping or loud swallowing are not only permissible, but expected.

Tanabata

On July 7 of every year, the nation celebrates the festival of the "weaver's earthly lover." The biggest celebrations are held in the Sendai area, when a clear sky at night is hoped for. This means that two stars that are in love with each other, but who are located at opposite ends of the milky way, can see each other. The story is from China and has many variations. The female, Star Weaver, visits earth and meets a young student, or shepherd, depending upon the version of the story. The heavenly king was angered with this visit, and ordered the weaver maiden never to return. Unrequited love is given universal attention on this festival day.

Tariffs

Tariffs are the surcharges that countries place on imported goods. Although Japan's tariffs are today at their lowest levels in modern history, the current friction between Japan and the U.S. and Europe is primarily due to tariffs and other barriers to trade.

From the Japanese point of view, the "country is open for marketing of foreign goods." Others say it is not open enough. The 1988 trade deficit between the U.S. and Japan was nearly 60 billion dollars. The U.S. claims that restrictions still exist impeding the sale of American goods and services in Japan, which creates the imbalance. Japan's vigorous inspection of foreign goods is considered one of the "non-tariff barriers" which are applied to agricultural products, drugs and medicines, and electro-mechanical appliances, including automobiles.

Japan's system of distribution is not well understood by many foreign businesses and, hence, is criticized as an intentional obstruction to a fair trade relationship. The U.S. Congress is addressing tensions caused by tarrifs and non-tariff barriers by passing legislation which would provide a more equitable exchange of market accessibility. The protectionist mood in the U.S. is intimidating the Japanese, who feel their superior products, selling well in European and American markets, are causing retaliatory action based on the concept of "reciprocity." America would deny trade opportunities to Japan to the same extent Japan denies America access to its markets. Japan has made efforts — some say not far reaching enough — to reduce the tariffs on most goods, including citrus and beef, and many non-trade barriers as well. The tariff-related economic tensions will continue to be the major issue betwen the U.S. and Japan for many years to come.

Tatemae And Honne

In the arena of communicating one's opinion or viewpoint, *tatemae* refers to a "formal stance" — even a facade — while *honne* is more indicative of one's true feelings or real position on a matter. In public and in group situations, Japanese rarely reveal their *honne*, but talk or present themselves in the "*tatemae* mode." At times, the presence of this dichotomy makes the Japanese appear duplicitous, especially in the eyes of Westerners. But given the structure of Japanese society, which is often described as "vertical" *(q.v.)*, where group harmony is of paramount importance, communicating by means of "*honne*," or naked frankness, would be to endanger relationships, causing frictions that may be difficult or impossible to eradicate. The group, therefore, does all it can to avoid such problems at the outset, and members communicate in a way which is known to be acceptable, with senior, respected persons taking the lead in discussing the essentials of a meeting, when necessary.

Taxes

See Also: TIPPING AND SERVICE CHARGES

There are both direct and indirect taxes which can be imposed on foreigners in Japan. A working foreign resident of a year or longer, or a non-resident who is paid money in Japan, pays income tax to both the national and local governments. For the resident and visiting foreigner alike, there are various consumer taxes on such items as travel, lodging, eating, drinking, and entertainment. In addition, certain commodities are taxed, including packaged liquor, tobacco, and many consumer goods such as electronic items, jewelry, clothing, and so forth. A 10% excise tax is applied to hotel, meals and drinks. If the bill for a hotel is under ¥4000 per night, or food and drink under ¥2000, the tax does not apply. The 15% service charge is included in the taxable amount. This corresponds to sales taxes in the U.S. of 8% or the VAT in Europe. Taxes on goods are exempt to foreigners with valid passports. Duty-free shops sell goods to consumers who must show proof of tax-free purchases upon leaving the country.

Taxis

Tokyo has nearly three times the number of taxis (some 30,000) as New York City. They are comfortable, clean, and safe. They can be hailed on the street, or engaged at designated spots in front of stations and hotels. A red light on the left side of the windshield indicates an unoccupied cab. One feature foreigners should be alerted to is the automatic door on the left side (traffic in Japan is on the left). When entering or exiting the taxi it is unnecessary to open or to close the door; the driver controls it.

Fares are ¥470 for the first 1.5 miles (2 km), then increasing by ¥80 or more (depending upon the taxi's size) for each additional one-fifth mile (370m). After 11 p.m. a 20% surcharge is added. When one has called a cab for pick-up, a light on the meter shows when the extra charge is in effect. For even later hours the percentage increases.

It is handy to have one's destination written in Japanese (as well as the place of return). The address alone will not do; the name of the destination building and/or section of town is needed. Addresses are rarely used in Japan except by the post office.

Tipping the drivers is not done; it is not in keeping with Japanese custom. One must be sure to distinguish a taxi — usually a bright color with name and company design boldly printed — from a "hire." The latter is very expensive, and akin to a private limousine in America.

Tea Ceremony

The *Cha-no-yu*, or tea ceremony, was imported from China in the late 8th Century (the Heian period) when tea was used as a medicine. Associated with Buddhism, in particular the Zen sects, tea became an elaborate activity and art form, its very preparation and consumption being highly formalized and philosophically regarded. Masters of the tea ceremony were revered as cult leaders, such as the great 16th Century master, Rikyu. Other leaders dating from the Muromachi era who lifted the ceremony to a cultured art leading to spiritual enrichment were Sho-o, Shinno, and Shuko.

Tea ceremony is practiced today in the same spirit, but has recreational and social elements as well. Despite the extremely complicated rules, social protocols and subtleties of motion demand of both servers and drinkers of the tea a calm approach to the ceremony. Young women today study the art to improve their skills in serving.

Tea House

There are literally millions of tea houses, called *kissaten*, all over Japan. In the country where there is a great shortage of living space and housing, people find *kissaten* as the replacement of a living room. One can sit over a cup of coffee for hours while listening to music, talking with friends, or simply reading materials one has brought in. There is a wide choice of *kissaten* in large cities; some with classical music, some with jazz, and some with dim lights and soft music catering exclusively to young lovers. The favored drink is coffee, which is usually very good and strong. It is expensive, but one pays for the space and ambience as well.

Telephones, Telex, And Telegrams

Service in Japan is fast and efficient. The Nippon Telegraph and Telephone Company (NTT) is a nationwide private corporation which mounts the service and controls the rates. The calls originating from Japan are more expensive than the same calls coming in from other countries, something to keep in mind when telephoning back to the States. Prearranging to receive calls, or communicating by either telegram or telex, is an economical move.

English language directories are available in hotels. Yellow pages are also available at large bookstores and in hotel rooms. Both operator-assisted and direct dialing (150) overseas is possible from Japan.

Within Japan, public telephones are readily available. Red telephones are for local and inter-city calls, and accept 10 coins, up to six at a time. Blue phones accept up to 10 coins, and are also used for local and inter-city calls; they are usually in booths. The yellow phones facilitate long distance calls and can handle up to nine ¥100 coins. Green phones accept pre-paid magnetic credit cards. The current rates for calls can be obtained from NTT. Large hotels maintain telegram and telex facilities. Telegrams to the U.S. are ¥118 for each word, regular service; ¥95 night letter.

For direct dialing from the U.S. to Japan, dial 011, then the prefix for Japan, 81, followed by the area code of the city desired. The lowest rate is between 3:00 A.M. and 2:00 P.M.: $2.38 for the first minute; $.89 (plus tax) for each additional minute. From 8:00 P.M. to 3:00 A.M.: $2.98 for one minute; $1.12 for each additional. From 2:00 P.M. to 8:00 P.M.: $3.96 for the first minute; $1.48 thereafter. Operator-assisted calls cost $8.87 for three minutes; $11.83 for person-to-person calls. The time difference in Japan is as follows:

U.S. Time Zones	EST	CST	MST	PST
Time Difference (in hours, in Japan)	+14	+15	+16	+17

(See Also: TIME ZONES)

For a complete list of area codes, please see the appendix.

Theater

See Also: ALL-GIRL REVUE; BUNRAKU; FILMS; KABUKI; NOH
In addition to traditional or classical Japanese theater, modern
theater is very much in evidence in the large urban areas of Japan.
Original Japanese plays, as well as translation of foreign plays, are
staged in a number of theaters, such as the Haiyu-za in Roppongi
(Tokyo).

Time Zones

Japan is on the same time all year round, with no daylight savings time
in effect. In addition, the entire country is in the same time zone.
Because Japan is the first major country west of the international date
line, all other countries are in later time zones. Hawaii is nineteen
hours behind Japan (10:00 a.m. in Japan is 3:00 p.m. the previous day
in Hawaii); Los Angeles and Seattle are seventeen hours behind;
Chicago, fifteen; and New York, fourteen (10:00 a.m. in Japan is 8:00
p.m. in New York the previous day). London and Paris are eight hours
behind Tokyo.

Tipping And Service Charges

Tipping is not necessary in Japan. Taxi drivers, waitresses, hotel porters, and the like are not tipped. At airports and railroad stations, a
standard charge per bag carried by porters is ¥250 or ¥300. Service
charges are automatically placed on bills at hotels and inns. In restaurants, for any charges of ¥2000 per person or more, the service
charge is assessed and included in the bill.

Tokyo

Tokyo is the capital of Japan and is the largest city, with a population
of more than 8,400,000. Because of urban sprawl, the population exceeds
11,000,000 when "greater Tokyo" is taken into consideration. The seat
of government, the hub of the financial world, the education nucleus —
all of these combine to form the busiest and fascinatingly modern city
of Japan. Tokyo means "Eastern Capital" and gets the designation in
contrast to Kyoto, the western capital of Japan for ten centuries. The
term "Edo" is associated with Tokyo as the early name for the
administration center established by the first Tokugawa Shogun in
1603.

Tokyo is ruled by an elected governor and a 125 member Metropolitan
Council. The city is divided into 23 wards (*ku*). An additional 26 cities
are part of the jurisdiction, and some satellite cities are "bedroom
communities" benefiting from Tokyo services and the business/
recreational environment it offers.

The top attractions for visitors in Tokyo are the Imperial Palace,
National Diet (Legislature), Meiji Shrine, Meiji Gallery, Akasaka

Detached Palace (official governmental guest house), Tokyo Tower, Ginza and Nihonbashi shopping streets, Yasukuni Shrine, Korakuen gardens and amusement park, Ueno Zoo and Park, and Asakusa Kannon Shrine. Sightseeing buses are available from Fujita Travel Service, Japan Travel Bureau, Japan Gray Line, Hato Bus, and others. Nighttime tours of entertainment spots are also available by contacting these tourist agencies or their representatives at major hotels. See appendix for a list of sightseeing companies.

The wards closest to the center of Tokyo are Chiyoda-ku and Minato-ku, in which most of the attractions are located. Subways offer an efficient and economical alternative to bus tours. There are ten lines criss-crossing frequently, making transfers possible and, sometimes, complicated. English maps of the subway are available at station offices.

Even by Japanese standards of population density, Tokyo is a monstrous entity, and due to the lack of straight, consistently intersecting streets, a maze. But getting around is safe and getting to know the city is easy. The real challenge (and rewards equal to it) is getting out into parts of Tokyo that are off the beaten track for most tourists.

The U.S. Embassy is centrally located and can be contacted for Consular assistance guaranteed all Americans. The address is 10-1 Akasaka, 1-Chome, Minato-ku.

Tokyo University

Japan's premier university, operated by the national government. It is as highly regarded as Harvard, Berkeley, Stanford, or Princeton in the U.S. The history of Tokyo University (usually called Todai) begins with the events related to the 1868 restoration of imperial rule in Japan. In 1869, when the nation's capital was moved from Kyoto to Tokyo, the new government absorbed the shogunate schools and made them government institutions. In 1870 the predecessor of Todai was formed into groups; their curricula consisted of studies in Japanese classics and Confucianism, together with Western sciences and medicine. Tokyo University was named as such in 1877, through the merger of two of the campuses having separate specialities. The purpose of the new university was to train the technical experts and government officials needed to modernize Japan.

Much has changed in the years since then. Today the university is located in campuses and sites all throughout the country, and has the largest budget of any of the some 70 national universities. Aspiring diplomats know that they must be accepted into Todai before they can begin to realize their hopes for government service. The main campus is located on the former estate of the Maeda family, in the Hongo area of Tokyo. The enrollment is under 20,000 students.

Tours And Tour Guides

See Also: MAJOR SITES

There are well-organized short-term and long-term tours available in Japan. In Tokyo, the daytime and Tokyo-by-night tours are popular among non-Japanese speaking visitors. They are reasonably priced (about ¥12,000 with dinner; ¥9000 without), well-paced, and greatly facilitate the travel, language, and timing needs of the newcomer. Information on and sign-up for these tours is available at the major hotels, where pick-up and drop-off occur. Prices vary according to the type of tour. There is always an English-speaking guide along and the buses are comfortable and safely driven.

Longer tours, with itineraries of one to three weeks, are also available. A typical one-week tour would include Tokyo, Nikko, Kamakura, Kyoto and Nara. Tours can be arranged before or after arrival in Japan. The Japan Travel Bureau, a quasi-governmental agency, has an eleven-day "Sunrise Holiday Tour" (about $2,700). Shorter periods of three, five, and eight days cost from $300 to $800. Some include all meals.

In the States, the Japan National Tourist Organization has offices in major cities to facilitate tour plans. Maps and brochures are free. In Japan, the Japanese Association of Travel Agents in Tokyo can be contacted for English language tour information. (See appendix.)

Trading Companies

Sogo-shosha, more commonly known as *shosha*, is a comprehensive "trading company," a Japanese innovation that has been the backbone of Japan's rapid expansion into the world market. A *shosha* does not simply export and import, but serves as an organizer and planner of large business and industrial projects by coordinating finances, manpower, raw materials, technology transfer, advertising, and so on. Thus a *shosha* is a multi-faceted organization, one that also plays a significant role domestically in guiding urban development, leisure industries, and environmental issues. Mitsui, Mitsubishi, Marubeni and C. Itoh are a few of the giant *shosha*.

Trains

See Also: TRANSPORTATION; BULLET TRAIN

The entire country is virtually accessible by train. More trains are available between points in and around the Eastern Seaboard corridor (Tokyo to Kobe) than elsewhere, and travel up and down the island of Honshu (*q.v.*) on the pacific side is more highly facilitated than travel across it.

Fares for trains are charged according to distance, speed, and accommodations. These separate charges may appear on a single ticket issued the traveler, or may be represented by separate tickets for each item. The Bullet Train (*q.v.*) offers the fastest and most luxurious train service in Japan. Tickets are collected at the end of a journey, and must be kept until the destination is reached.

In addition to Express and Limited Express trains for long distance runs, rapid service also exists within and between cities and suburbs. Trains have diners, sleepers, recliners, snacks, alcoholic beverage service, etc., depending upon distance and need for such accommodations. English language announcements are provided on selected routes popular among foreigners. First class service is referred to as "Green Car" class and on the major runs is recognizable by the green four-leaf clovers on the side. Current prices for Green Car and Regular class service can be found in the appendix.

Bullet Train tickets cannot be purchased in the United States, but some travel agencies can reserve them when booking flights to Japan.

Railpass purchases are available before arrival in Japan only. For information write Nippon Travel Service in New York (212/986-7393), or any Japan National Tourist Organization (JNTO) office abroad. Note: For transportation information to and from airports, see appendix.

Transportation

See Also: TRAINS; AIRLINES; TAXIS

Urban, suburban, and inter-city travel is highly efficient, well-developed, and very crowded in large cities, to and from popular sightseeing areas, and on high speed trains along the Eastern Seaboard. Expansion of high speed service to areas in central and northern Japan is under way. Japan Railways Group (JR), formerly Japan National Railways (JNR), serves as the major source of transportation for the travelling public, and it provides train, bus, and sea service. The use of private autos is increasing and along with it, road traffic over improved roadways is growing. High speed toll roads link Tokyo and Kobe, and other major traffic corridors in Japan. In addition to private autos, trucking lines add to the congestion of the highway system.

The now privatized JR is the backbone of the transportation network. It has more than 5000 railway stations on the four main islands. Seven of the nation's busiest stations are in Tokyo, with two in Osaka, and one in Yokohama. JR pricing has increased markedly in the past years, and for intra-urban travel, the public often chooses from the cheaper rail services available.

For the foreigner, trains are easier to use than buses or self-driven autos. The train stations are invariably shown in both native Japanese characters as well as romanized equivalents. Bus stops and highway signs rarely carry instructions or place names that foreigners who have no knowledge of Kanji or Kana can read. Streetcars are all but extinct, but subway travel is very active in Tokyo, Osaka, Yokohama, Sapporo, and Nagoya. Subway travel offers the fastest and most reliable means of transportation in these cities.

Ship passenger services, including car ferries, are in operation throughout the country. Hydrofoil boats are found in tourist and recreation areas.

Japan has three major airline companies (See Airlines), Japan Airlines (JAL), All-Nippon Airways, and Japan Air system, formerly Toa Domestic Airlines. A fourth, local carrier service, is the Southwest Airlines (SWAL), which operates out of Okinawa Prefecture and provides inter-island connections. Japan's 65 airports are under the administration of either the Ministry of Transport's Civil Aviation Bureau, or are operated by local authorities. The major airports (*q.v.*) are Narita International, Haneda International, and Osaka International.

U

Ueno

Located in the northern section of Tokyo, this thriving satellite offers a major railway station for travel to northern Japan, a park with a beautiful pond and splendid cherry blossoms, a musical festival center, the Tokyo National Museum, the Tokyo Metropolitan Art Gallery, one of the oldest libraries in Japan, and a zoo. There are also shrines, department stores, movie houses, restaurants, and night spots to round out the variety of attractions offered by this neighbor of Asakusa, the traditional playground of old Tokyo. The Tobu Line leaves Ueno for Nikko.

Universities

There are seven main national universities in Japan, the foremost of which is the University of Tokyo (1877). It is followed by Kyoto University (1897), Tohoku University in Sendai (1907), Kyushu University in Fukuoka (1910), Hokkaido University in Sapporo (1918), Osaka University (1931), and Nagoya University (1939). There are other national and prefectural universities, but they are not in league with the seven former imperial universities. Private universities and colleges bring the total number in Japan to nearly 500, with a total student body of nearly 1.9 million. The prestigious private universities include Keio, founded in 1859, and Waseda; other notable private universities are Meiji, Rikkyo, Hosei, and Nihon; Sophia and International Christian University offer courses in English.

V

Vertical Society

Human relations within a group are usually organized on the basis of either horizontal or vertical frames. A horizontal relationship is predicated upon relative equality of the members of the group, while a vertical relationship assumes the existence of the superior-inferior hierarchy among the members. Most groups in Japan, including business firms and educational institutions, are primarily vertically organized. Within a company, for example, there is a clear-cut and unchangeable "pecking order," usually based on the length of service. One aspect of the Japanese vertical organization is that a superior is obligated to care for an inferior in return for the inferior's serving the superior — no doubt a legacy of the not-so-distant feudal past. In modern terms, the typical human relationship in Japan may be described as a patron-client relationship.

Members of a vertically oriented society always tend to see themselves as either superior or inferior to someone. Thus, even among siblings within a Japanese family, there is a sense of ranking, according to their ages. Internationally, Japanese tend to regard themselves either above or below (rarely equal to) other nations in terms of their worldwide rank and ability. Japan has historically regarded herself alternately superior and inferior to the U.S. The 1990's may see the start of Japan's "superiority complex" coming to the fore.

Wood Block Prints

Names like Harunobu, Utamaro, Sharaku, Toyokuni, Hokusai, and Hiroshige are familiar to wood block print enthusiasts the world over. The giants of the medium flourished in the 18th Century and brought to the genre a common appeal, with scenes which merchant, townsman, and samurai alike could relate to. Known in Japanese as the *Ukiyoe*, or "picture of the floating world," the prints are available for viewing in museums and palaces; reproductions of the famous "Fifty-three stations of Tokaido," by Hiroshige, and Kabuki personalities, Geisha, etc. are available for a few thousand yen today in most of the shopping arcades in Tokyo, Osaka, Kyoto, and Nagoya. Yet, *Ukiyoe* are not the only wood block prints. *Mokuhan* is the wood block from which earliest writings were produced in mass quantities. Many authors and artists have used the process since the 6th Century, in China; since the 8th Century in Japan. It was the medium used before (and after) moveable type to transmit literature, art and religious documents.

Y

Yakuza

A Japanese functional counterpart to the *cosa nostra* gangster organizations in America and elsewhere. Members of the *yakuza* organizations are often identifiable by their colorful and extensive tattoos. One sees in movies and popular literature a romanticized version of the yakuza's supposed samurai virtues of loyalty, compassion and brotherly love. But they are known to be engaged in gambling, extortion, weapons and drug traffic.

'Yes' And 'No' In Japanese

Japanese-English dictionaries and grammars define "hai" as "yes" and "iie" as "no." "Hai" is a word of assent. It is also used to show that one understands what the speaker is saying. "Hai" means "Yes, sir" or "Yes, ma'am," rather than just "Yes." The use of these two words (or interjections) is the same as their usage in English. For example: "Eiga ni ikimasu ka?" ("Are you going to the movies?") "Hai. Ikimasu." ("Yes. I am going.") Also: "Iie. Ikimasen." ("No. I am not going.") However, in certain uses, the opposite meaning may be intended, depending upon how a question is put. For example: "Kino, eiga ni ikimasen deshita ka?" ("Didn't you go to the movies yesterday?") "Hai. Ikimasen deshita." ("No. I did not go.") Literally, "Yes, that's correct. I did not go." "Hai," therefore, can mean "That's right" or "What you have said is correct," and "iie" can indicate that what is spoken "is incorrect." When the question posed is in a negative mode, the standard response is made to the form rather than the substance of the question. Likewise, "iie" can be used to mean "yes." For example: "Doko e mo ikimasen deshita ka?" ("Didn't you go anywhere?") "Iie. Eiga ni ikimashita." ("Yes. I went to the movies.") Literally, "That is incorrect. I did go to the movies." As an interjection, then, "hai" can mean that one understands what the speaker has said, or that "the message is received; or is understood" — but not necessarily agreed to. The less formal equivalent of "hai" is "eh." "Haa" also is a variation of "hai." These utterances are used by the Japanese to indicate an agreeable attitude. They serve other important social functions as well and are often present, even when the Japanese speak English.

Another important social aspect of "yes" and "no" in Japan relates to the hesitancy to say "no" outright. There are many ways of avoiding any direct answer, especially an unpleasant one. "No" is rarely used to contradict someone, but is used, for example, to deny one's own accomplishments, refuse a compliment, etc. The foreign speaker should be careful not to confuse "hai" with agreement. While it may in fact mean "yes," one has to listen carefully. The speaker may just be saying, "I am hearing you, and you have my attention."

Yokohama

The second largest city in Japan, and the largest seaport, handling traffic from the U.S. (Kobe is second.) Approximately 2,800,000 people call Yokohama "home." Just a 19 minute ride on the Bullet Train from Tokyo, the Yokohama area blends with the urbanization known as "Greater Tokyo." Yet, there is much to give distinction to this city. It has a port town flavor to it, with sections devoted to Westerners (The Bluff), Chinese food (Chinatown), traditional shopping (Motomachi), theaters and shopping (Isezaki-cho), and others. As the prefectural seat of Kanagawa, there are governmental, educational, sports and music hall facilities throughout the city. Yokohama has excellent restaurants, museums, hotels, hospitals, transportation, and shopping. Yet, it lives in the shadow of Tokyo, which has usurped its role as the first Japanese soil onto which the foreigner trod. It is now relegated to passing mention by the tour guide on the way to Kamakura. The visitor to Yokohama should try to see the Sojiji Temple and the Sankei-en, two superlative examples of 14th Century temple architecture and Tokugawa landscape gardening, respectively.

Z

Zaibatsu

Literally, "wealth clique." Such great industrial and financial conglomerates as Mitsui, Mitsubishi, Sumitomo, and Yasuda were based on family wealth which grew into combinations of inter-related families. Before World War II, *zaibatsu* combines were directed at the top by holding companies, which were outlawed after the War. These companies have survived the Occupation-imposed restrictions by maintaining looser ties, but the binding nature of their relationships in non-organizational terms continues. The directors of companies, now forbidden by law to be *zaibatsu*, still meet together through bonds of friendship, inter-company loans, interlocking directorships, common stock, and other forms of mutual assistance. Today the dominant role within the tight group is played by the trading company (*q.v.*) or a bank; or both. Mitsui, Mitsubishi, and Sumitomo are still the big three giants among the some ten large trading companies involved in networks of worldwide purchase and selling. These are not, strictly speaking, *zaibatsu* in the pre-War sense, because cartelization has been taken over in Japan by the government and a new integration of commercial power has resulted.

JAPANESE LANGUAGE BASICS

Now that you've had the chance to read over the topics that interest you the most in *Japan Today*, take this opportunity to introduce yourself to the Japanese language.

By listening to the cassette, you will learn words and expressions that you can use in day-to-day business situations with Japanese clients and during your next trip to Japan.

You will also receive instruction on how to pronounce Japanese words and names and get a feel for Japanese sentence structure. In addition, we'll be giving you pointers on Japanese business etiquette.

PRONOUNCING JAPANESE WORDS

You may be surprised to hear that compared to English, Japanese is really a very simple language to speak. One of the reasons is that there are relatively few new sounds to learn. In fact, English has many more different ways of pronouncing vowels and consonants than Japanese does.

For example, how many different ways do we pronounce the letter "a"? There's "ay," as in *favor,* "ae," as in *after*, and "ah," as in *father*, just to name three. In alphabetized—or Romanized—Japanese, there is only one pronunciation: the letter "a" is always pronounced "ah." This greatly simplifies pronunciation.

Note: A cassette tape is available containing the language material on the following pages.

Here's a trivia question. Who was the Japanese partner of the old radio hero the Green Hornet? The answer is spelled K-A-T-O. How would we pronounce K-A-T-O in Japanese? We say Kato (Kah-toh), not Kato (Kay-toh), as it was incorrectly pronounced in the show. In English, there are different ways to pronounce K-A-T-O, but in Japanese there is only one. This makes pronunciation very easy.

Since "Kato" is a very common Japanese name and you're likely to be meeting somebody with that name, chances are you've already improved your Japanese relations skills.

And that's the point of this tape. By learning a little about correct pronunciation of names, and by taking the time and effort to learn a few basic daily expressions of welcome, a few greetings, and responses, we show our Japanese hosts and guests that we are interested in them and in their culture. By demonstrating this interest, you're likely to find your business transactions going a little more smoothly, and you may even make friends in the process.

Now, listen carefully to the pronunciation of Japanese vowels.

As we said, "a" is always pronounced "ah," as in the English word *father*.

The letter "i" is always pronounced "ee," as in *sheep*.

The letter "u" is always pronounced "oo," as in *pool*.

The letter "e" is always pronounced "eh," as in *pet*.

The final vowel, the letter "o," is always pronounced "o," as in *alone*.

There you have them: there are only five vowel sounds in Japanese.

"A" is pronounced "ah."

"I" is pronounced "ee."

"U" is pronounced "oo."

"E" is pronounced "eh."

"O" is pronounced "o."

A, i, u, e, o.

In many Japanese words, there are two identical vowel sounds next to each other, like "a a." We pronounce this by briefly lengthening the sound of the vowel. Often this difference is imperceptible to the Western ear. However, the slight difference in pronunciation can have a significant effect on the meaning of the word. For example, can you tell the difference between the words "obasan" and "obaasan?" Listen again. Obasan . . . obaasan. In the second word, the "ah" sound is held a little longer. It might seem to be a minor difference, however, the first word means *aunt* and the second word means *grandmother.*

One more point: when you read an "a" and an "i" together, pronounce it like the English letter "i." Actually, it's the same way we pronounce the "a" and "i" in our word *aisle.* "A" and "i" together are pronounced "i."

In a similar way, many Japanese words have a double consonant sound. This will be represented in a romanized alphabet by two consonants in a row. For example, a double "p" sound in "koppu" (*glass*); a double "t" sound in "chotto" (*a little*); a double "s" sound in "kissaten" (*tea house*); and a double "k" sound in "hakkiri" (*clearly*).

Now let's practice your new Japanese pronunciation skills by going over the names of Japan's major islands and cities. Besides reviewing the basic vowel sounds, you'll discover that Japanese consonants are pronounced very similarly to ours.

EXERCISE

Four Major Islands

Hokkaido	Kyushu
Honshu	Shikoku

Major Cities

Hiroshima	Niigata	Kobe
Kitakyushu	Sapporo	Kyoto
Kagoshima	Sendai	Osaka
Nagasaki	Tokyo	Yokohama
Nagoya		

JAPANESE GREETINGS

Let's look at some basic Japanese greetings and the time of day they should be used.

If you greet a Japanese person early in the morning before, 10 A.M., you would say, "Ohayo gozaimasu." Remember, "ohayo gozaimasu" means *good morning*.

If you greet a Japanese person after that time, you say, "Konnichiwa," which means, *Good morning*, or *Good day*.

If you meet a Japanese person in the evening, you would greet him by saying, "Kombanwa." This means *Good evening*.

Let's review. "Ohayo gozaimasu" is said before 10:00 A.M. and means *good morning*. "Konnichiwa" is said after 10:00 A.M. and means *good day* or *good morning*. Finally, "Kombanwa" means *good evening*.

To say goodbye at the end of the day, you use a word that you are probably already familiar with: "sayonara."

Another way to say *goodbye* is "Ja mata." "Ja mata" means *See you later*.

INTRODUCTIONS

Now let's learn the expressions to use when being introduced to a Japanese person. These apply when you are being introduced in a business setting, and when you are making the acquaintance of a new friend.

In English, when we meet someone for the first time, typically we say, "Nice to meet you" and "How do you do?" The Japanese say "Hajimemashite" and "Dozo Yoroshiku."

"Hajimemashite" expresses the desire for a good beginning to the relationship. "Dozo yoroshiku" expresses the hope that the new acquaintances will help each other.

"Hajimemashite" is said first. "Dozo yoroshiku" is said after one has said one's name.

In addition to saying your name, you should be ready at the time of introduction to exchange business cards. Note that in Japan one exchanges business cards, or "meishi," as the Japanese call them, at the beginning of the meeting or acquaintance. This helps in learning a new name and in identifying a business person's rank and status in a company.

DINING OUT

Here are a few expressions that you might find useful when dining with Japanese business acquaintances or friends.

When raising their glasses in a toast, the Japanese say, "Kampai!" which means *Cheers!*

One never pours one's own drink in Japan. But, you should take special care to refill the glass of your dinner companions. If your friend moves to refill your glass when you've had enough, just say, "Kekkoo desu," which means, *That's enough; I don't care for any more.*

If you find the food very delicious, what would say say? "Totemo oishii desu." "Totemo" means *very*. "Oishii" means *delicious*. And "desu" is the Japanese word for *is*.

In saying "Totemo oishii desu," you've said an entire sentence in Japanese. Let's take this opportunity to see how different from English the typical Japanese word order is.

JAPANESE WORD ORDER

In an English sentence, the usual word order is subject-verb-object, as in "I like movies," or "She writes letters." In Japanese, the order of the ideas is different. The verb always comes at the end of the sentence. And very often, the doer of the action, the subject, is entirely left out. Japanese assume, for example, that since I am here, and I say "enjoy movies," you can generally figure out that it's I who enjoys them.

"Desu," meaning *is*, is the last word of our sentence "Totemo oishii desu." And the subject of the sentence, the food, is left out. All that is said is "Very delicious is," but we get the meaning. Even with the subject left out and the verb coming at the end of the sentence, the Japanese communicate very accurately and efficiently.

REQUESTS AND THANK YOUS

One Japanese word for *please* is "dōzo." "Dōzo" is said when asking someone to accept something. For example, if you held a door open for someone else to enter before you, you might smile and say "Dōzo," meaning *please go ahead of me*.

The Japanese for *thank you* is "dōmo arigatō," or just "dōmo" in less formal situations. Since the Japanese are very formal and polite in business situations and with guests, chances are you'll hear "dōmo arigatō" quite often.

If someone thanks you, the correct reply in Japanese is "Dō itashimashite," meaning *you're welcome*.

OTHER USEFUL EXPRESSIONS

So far you have learned: Japanese pronunciation; greetings; introductions; how to exchange business cards; and words you might use when dining out. Now let's learn a few other useful Japanese expressions.

One that you will undoubtedly hear and might want to use is "sumimasen." "Sumimasen" means *excuse me*.

Here's an expression that is unique to Japanese culture and etiquette: "Shitsurei shimasu." In essence, this phrase expresses apology for rudeness. What is interesting about this expression is that the Japanese, who are extremely polite, say "shitsurei shimasu" on occasions that most Westerners would not consider rude at all.

For example, you would say "shitsurei shimasu" on entering someone else's home, when passing in front of someone, or when leaving the room in the middle of a meeting. You might say it's a special form of *pardon me*. Some Japanese say "shitsurei shimasu" when leaving after a visit, almost like saying *Pardon me for leaving now.*

Yes in Japanese is simply, "hai." By the way, "hai" doesn't always mean agreement. Much of the time, when a Japanese person nods and repeats, "hai," he is merely indicating that he is listening to your words and trying to follow along with your meaning.

And while we're on the subject of agreement and disagreement, we should note that for cultural reasons, more traditional Japanese are hesitant to say no, especially to a request. Again, the Japanese politeness and eagerness to please are apparent. Still, when the situation is appropriate, the word for *no* is "iie."

If you're shopping in a Japanese store and would like to ask what a certain item costs, you would say, "Sore wa ikura desu ka?" "Sore wa" means *that object.* "Ikura" means *how much.* "Desu" means *is*, and the presence of the word "ka" indicates that a question is being asked. "Sore wa ikura desu ka." *That object how much is*? or *How much is that*?

In many situations in a foreign country, a person can become lost or confused. If you don't understand what is being said, you might say, "Wakarimasen," *I don't understand.*

On a more positive note, when you have understood what is being said, just say, "wakarimashita," *I understand.*

Now let's listen to some basic, everyday Japanese words and phrases.

GREETINGS AND COMMON EXPRESSIONS

Good morning.
Ohayō
(casual)
Ohayō gozaimasu.

Good afternoon/Hello.
Kon'nichiwa.

Good evening.
Kon'banwa.

Good night.
Oyasumi.
(casual)
Oyasuminasai.

Good-bye.
Sayōnara.

See you again.
Ja mata.
(casual)
Mata oaishimashō.

Take care of yourself.
Ogenki de.

How have you been?
Ogenki desu ka?.

I've been fine, thank you.
Okage sama de, genki desu.

Thank you.
Arigatō.
(casual)
Arigatō gozaimasu.
(before a favor is granted).
Arigāto gozaimashita.
(after a favor is done)

You're welcome.
Dō itashimashite.

Welcome.
(to the house)
Irasshaimase.

No need to worry .
Goshimpai naku.

It's O.K./I'm O.K.
Daijōbu desu.

Are you O.K.?
Daijōbu desu ka?

Pleased to meet you.
Dōzo yoroshiku.

Give my best to ___.
_____-san ni yoroshiku.

Congratulations!
Omedetō.
(casual)
Omedetō gozaimasu.

Excuse me.
Sumimasen.
Shitsurei shimasu.

I'm sorry.
Gomen'nasai.

BASIC EXPRESSIONS

General

Yes
Hai; Ee;   Un
(casual) (very casual)

No
Iie

Yes, it is.; That's right.
Hai, sō desu.

Is that right?
Sō desu ka?

Please.; Help yourself.
Dōzo.

That's fine.
Ii desu.; Kekkō desu.
(polite)

102

I; me
Watashi

You
Anata

Will you say it again?
Mō ichido itte kudasai?

I don't know.
Shirimasen.

I don't understand.
Wakarimasen.

Introduction and Visits

What is your name, please?
Shitsurei desu ga, onamae wa?

I am _____.
Watashi wa _____ to mōshimasu.

Where are you from?
Dochira kara irasshai-mashita ka?

Where are you headed?
Dochira e irasshaimasu ka?

May I see (or talk to)

Mr. Yoshida?
Yoshida-san o onegai shimasu.

Please wait a moment.
Shōshō omachi kudasai.

Thank you for waiting.
Dōmo omachidō sama.

Please come this way.
Dōzo kochira e.

It's been a while.
Hisashiburi desu ne.

Eating and Drinking

Are you thirsty?
Nodo ga kawaki mashita ka?

What would you like to drink?
Nani o nomimasu ka?

Would you like some coffee?
Kōhī wa ikaga desu ka?

Please give me some tea.
Ocha o onegai shimasu.

Are you hungry?
Onaka ga sukimashita ka?

It's delicious!
Oishii desu ne.

Give me some beer.
Biiru o kudasai./Biiru o onegaishimasu.

On the street, in Taxis

Excuse me, but...
Shitsurei desuga...

Where is the station?
Eki wa doko desu ka?

Tokyo station, please.
Tōkyō-eki (made) onegaishimasu.

Where am I?/What place is this?
Koko wa doko desu ka?

Stop here, please.
Koko de tomatte kudsai.

Turn right (left), please.
Migi (hidari) ni magatte kudasai.

Go straight, please.
Massugu itte kudasai.

Is it far (near)?
Tōi (Chikai) desu ka?

Please call a taxi.
Takushii o yonde kudasai.

Shopping

How much?
Ikura desu ka?

Thank you for waiting.
Omachidō sama.

Please give this (that) to me.
Kore (Sore/Are) o kudasai.

That's expensive, isn't it.
Takai desu ne.

That's inexpensive.
Yasui desu.

Wrap them, please.
Tsutsunde kudasai.

Will you send it?
Okutte kudasaimasen ka?

My address is _____.
Watashi no jūsho wa ____.

Where is the telephone?
Denwa wa doko desu ka?

NUMBERS
Sino-Japanese System

0–rei, (zero)	7–shichi (nana)	20–ni-jū
1–ichi	8–hachi	21–ni-jū-ichi
2–ni	9–kyū	22–ni-jū-ni
3–san	10–jū	
4–shi (yon, yo)	11–jū-ichi	30–san-jū
5–go	12–jū-ni	100–hyaku
6–roku ·	13–jū-san	101–hyaku-ichi

111–hyaku-jū-ichi

159–hyaku-go-jū-kyū

200–ni-hyaku
300–san-byaku
400–yon-hyaku
500–go-hyaku

1,000–sen

1,983–sen-kyu-hyaku-hachi-ju-san
10,000–ichi-man
16,500–ichi-man-roku-sen-go-hyaku

Traditional Japanese System

1–hitotsu	6–muttsu
2–futatsu	7–nanatsu
3–mittsu	8–yattsu
4–yottsu	9–kokonotsu
5–itsutsu	10–tō

EXERCISE

How much is this?
Kore wa ikura desu ka?

It's 250 yen.
Ni-hyaku-go-jū en desu.

CONCLUSION

Through this book and cassette, you have had your first exposure to the Japanese language. You know the basic pronunciation of Japanese vowels, useful expressions, and a little about the etiquette involved in daily life. Of course, we have barely skimmed the surface of Japanese culture. But we hope that you have gotten your feet wet, and that your curiosity is stirred to find out more.

And here's one last Japanese expression. It's used to encourage people and to cheer them on. It means *Please do your best.* "Gambatte kudasai." We urge you to enjoy *Japan Today* and hope that it deepens your knowledge and interest in this important culture. "Gambatte kudasai!"

SELECTED BIBLIOGRAPHY

General

Christopher, Robert C. *The Japanese Mind: The Goliath Explained.* New York: Linden Press/Simon & Schuster, 1983.

Doi, Takeo. *The Anatomy of Dependence.* Tr. by John Bester. Tokyo, New York: Kodansha International, 1973. 170 p.

Lebra, Takie Sugiyama. *Japanese Patterns of Behavior.* Honolulu: Univ. of Hawaii Press, 1976. 295 p.

Nakane, Chie. *Japanese Society.* Berkeley: Univ. of California Press, 1970. 157 p.

Reischauer, Edwin O. *The Japanese,* Cambridge, Belknap Press, 1977. 443 p.

Sansom, George B. *Japan; A Short Cultural History.* Rev. ed. London: Cresset Press, 1952. 548 p.

Vogel, Ezra F. *Japan As Number One: Lessons for America.* Cambridge, Harvard Univ. Press, 1979. 272 p.

Business

Business and Society in Japan. Reports of a Study of Japanese Business. Ed. by Bradley M. Richardson and Taizo Ueda. New York: Praeger, 1981. 334 p.

Clark, Rodney. *The Japanese Company.* New Haven: Yale Univ. Press, 1979. 282 p.

De Mente, Boye. *How to Do Business With The Japanese.* Lincolnwood, IL: NTC Publishing Group, 1989. 256p.

Gibney, Frank B. *Miracle by Design: The Real Reasons Behind Japan's Economic Success.* New York: Times Books, 1983. 256 p.

Graham, John L. and Yoshihiro Sano. *Smart Bargaining: Doing Business with the Japanese.* Cambridge: Ballinger Publishing, 1984. 165 p.

Noda, Yosiyuki. *Introduction to Japanese Law.* Tr. and ed. by Anthony H. Angelo. Tokyo: Univ. of Tokyo Press, 1976. 253 p.

Language

Ahlberg, R. and T. Ando, et al. *Just Enough Japanese.* Lincolnwood, IL: National Textbook Co., 1985. 190 p.

Association for Japanese-Language Teaching. *Japan for Busy People.* Tokyo: Kodansha International Ltd., 1984.

Kenkyusha's New Little Japanese-English Dictionary. Ed. by T. Iwasaki. Tokyo: Kenkyusha. 1972, 550 p.

Mizutani, Osamu and Nobuko Mizutani. *An Introduction To Modern Japanese.* Tokyo: Japan Times, 1977. 425 p.

Schwarz, Edward A. and Reiko Ezawa. *Everyday Japanese.* Lincolnwood, IL: National Textbook Co., 1985. 208 p.

Vaccari, Oreste and Enko Elisa Vaccari. *The New Up-To-Date English-Japanese Conversation Dictionary.* Tokyo: Vaccari's Language Institute, 1974. 498 p.

Travel

Booth, Alan. *Japan: Land of Many Faces.* Lincolnwood, IL: Passport Books, 1988. 256 p.

De Mente, Boye. *Discovering Cultural Japan.* Lincolnwood, IL: Passport Books, 1988. 160 p.

De Mente, Boye. *Japan at Night.* Lincolnwood, IL: Passport Books, 1988. 320 p.

De Mente, Boye. *Japan Made Easy.* Lincolnwood, IL: Passport Books, 1989. 256 p.

Fisher, Robert C. *Japan 1985.* (Fisher annotated travel guides) New York: Fisher Travel Guides, 1985. 407 p.

Fodor's Japan 1985. New York: Fodor's Modern Guides, 1985. 534 p.

Japan National Tourist Organization. *Japan: The New Official Guide.* Tokyo: Japan Travel Bureau, 1975. 1088 p.

APPENDIX
Airlines (Reservations)

(All Tokyo Numbers)

Aeroflot Soviet Airlines	434-9671	Japan Asia Airways	455-7511
Air Canada	586-3891	K.L.M.	216-0771
Air France	475-1511	Korean Air Lines	211-3311
Air India	214-1981	LOT Polish	
Air Nauru	581-9271	Airlines	437-5741
Air New Zealand	287-1641	Lufthansa	580-2111
Alitalia	580-2181	Malaysian	503-5961
American Airlines	214-2111	Northwest	432-6000
Ansett	214-6876	Pakistan	
Australian Airlines	216-5828	International	216-6511
Austrian Airlines	582-2231	Pan American	
British Airways	214-4161	World Airways	508-2211
C.P. Air	212-5811	Philippines Airlines	593-2421
Canadian Airlines	281-7426	Qantas Airways	212-1351
Cathay Pacific	504-1531	Sabena	585-6151
China Airlines	436-1661	Scandinavia	
Continental Airlines	592-1731	Airlines	503-8101
Micronesia	592-1631	Singapore Airlines	213-3431
Delta Airlines	213-8781	South African	
Eastern Airlines	592-1634	Airways	470-1901
Egypt Air	211-4525	Swissair	212-1016
Ethiopian Airlines	281-1990	Thai Airways	503-3311
Finnair	580-9231	Transworld Airlines	212-1477
Garuda Indonesian		United Airlines	817-4411
Airways	593-1181	UTA	593-0773
Hawaiian Airlines	214-4774	Varig	211-6751
Iberia	582-3831	Western Airlines	213-2777
Iran Air	586-2101	World Airways	440-2238
Iraqi Airways	586-5801	Yugoslav Airways	434-3843
Japan Airlines	455-1121		

Domestic Airlines

All Nippon Airways	552-6311
Japan Air Lines	456-2111
Japan Air System Airlines	747-8111

Airports

Air Baggage Service Co.

Delivery service between hotel and airport for passengers with excess luggage.

Phone: (03) 543-8891

Baggage Pickup Service

One item @ 30 kgs or less	¥1500
Each add'l bag @ 30 kgs or less	¥1,000

Porter or Redcaps

Per piece of luggage	¥250 to ¥300

Departure Tax on International Flights

Adults	¥2000
Children under 12 years of age	¥1000

Baby Sitters

Ai Baby Sitters	930-0504
Baby Life Center	469-7387
Tokyo Domestic Service	584-4769

Bullet Train

Tokyo to Hakata in northern Kyushu (6 hrs and 45 min./730 miles)
Stops at: Nagoya
Kyoto
Shin-Osaka
Okayama
Hiroshima
Kokura

¥ 28,000 (one way)

Doctors and Dentists

Hibiya Clinic	502-2681
St. Luke's Hospital	541-5151
Tokyo Medical and Surgical Clinic	436-3028
Tokyo Sanitarium Hospital	392-6151
The Bluff Hospital (Yokohama)	045-641-6961
Japan Baptist Hospital (Kyoto)	075-781-5191
Yodogawa Christian Hosp. in Osaka	06-322-2250
Oyama Dental Clinic (Hotel New Otani)	265-1111
Olympia Ohba Dental Clinic	409-7155
Japan-American Dental Clinic	251-7555

Emergency Phone - Language Assistance

Tokyo Area	502-1461
Kyoto Area	(075) 371-5649

Outside of above areas dial 106 and tell operator in English "Collect Call, T.I.C." (Tourist Information Center)

Hotels in Tokyo and Osaka

(**03** when calling from outside to Tokyo; **06** from outside to Osaka)

Okura Hotel	582-0111	Royal Hotel	448-1121
Imperial Hotel	504-1111	Plaza Hotel	453-1111
Tokyo Hilton	344-5111	Grand Hotel	202-1212
New Otani	265-1111	Hotel Hanshin	344-1661
Keio Plaza	344-0111	Dai-Ichi	341-4411
Akasaka Prince	234-1111	Miyako	779-1501
Ana Hotel	505-1111	Osaka Airport	855-4621
Ginza Tokyu	541-2411	Osaka Tokyu	373-2411
Ginza Dai-Ichi	542-5311	Shin Hankyu	372-5101

Medical Insurance

Eisei Byoin (Sanitarium Hospital)	392-6151

Eisei Byoin is the Tokyo representative of the International Association

for Medical Assistance to Travelers.
(Headquarters in New York City.)

There is a listing for Kyoto and
Osaka as well.

Pharmacies

American Pharmacy in Yurakucho   271-4034
  (Hibiya Bldg.)

Restaurants

Chinzanso
943-1111
Ghenghis Khan style barbeque in a lovely setting of gardens and
tea houses.

Happoen
443-3111
Tempura, sukiyaki and other traditional dishes. Extensive gardens
of a former mansion surround the restaurant.

Edogin
543-4401
Superb sushi. Near the Tsukiji market, the freshest fish in town is
served in one of three separate little shops.

Furusato
463-2310
Folk style cooking with a floor show of dance and folk music.

Tenichi
571-1949
Quality tempura.

Zakuro
582-6841
Try the mizutaki, shabu-shabu, or sukiyaki.

Shopping

Department Stores

Ginza
Hankyu (Sukiyabashi)	573-2231
Komatsu	572-5151
Matsuya	567-1211
Matsuzakaya	572-1111
Meitetsu Melsa	567-2131
Mitsukoshi	562-1111
Sogo (Yurakucho)	284-6711
Wako	562-2111

Ikebukuro
Mitsukoshi	987-1111
Seibu	981-0111
Tobu	981-2211

Nihombashi
Daimaru (Tokyo Station)	212-8011
Mitsukoshi	241-3311
Takashimaya	211-4111
Tokyu	211-0511

Shibuya
Seibu	462-0111
Tokyu	477-3111

Shinjuku
Isetan	352-1111
Keio	342-2111
Mitsukoshi	354-1111
Odakyu	342-1111

Ueno, Asakusa
Keisei	835-2222
Matsuya	842-1111
Matsuzakaya	832-1111

Arcades
Handicraft Center	761-5080
International Arcade	591-2746
Japan Taxfree Center	432-4351
Nikkatsu Arcade	271-4527
Palace Hotel Shopping Arcade	211-5211
Sukiyabashi Shopping Center	571-0495

Sightseeing Companies

Fujita Travel Service	573-1011
Hato Bus	593-1083
Japan Gray Line	433-4801
Japan Travel Bureau	276-7777

Telephone Area Codes

City	Code	City	Code
Aizu Wakamatsu	2422	Kurashiki	864
Akashi	78	Kure	823
Akita (Akita)	188	Kyoto	75
Amagasaki	6	Maebashi	272
Aomori	177	Matsue	852
Asahigawa	166	Matsumoto	263
Ashikaga	284	Matsuyama	899
Beppu	977	Morioka	196
Chiba	472	Muroran	143
Chigasaki	467	Nagano	262
Chofu	424	Nagasaki	958
Fuchu (Tokyo)	423	Nagoya	52
Fukushima	245	Naha	988
Funabashi	474	Nara	742
Gifu	582	Niigata	252
Hachinohe	178	Nishinomiya	798
Hachioji	426	Numazu	559
Hakodate	138	Odawara	465
Hamamatsu	534	Oita	975
Himeji	792	Okayama	862
Hiratsuka	463	Osaka	6
Hirosaki	172	Otaru	134
Hiroshima	822	Sapporo	11
Ichikawa	473	Sasebo	956
Ichinomiya		Sendai	222
(Chiba)	47542	Shimonoseki	832
Ise	596	Tachikawa	425
Itami	727	Takamatsu	878
Iwakuni	827	Takarazuka	797
Kagoshima	992	Takasaki	273
Kamakura	467	Tokushima	886
Kawasaki	44	Tokyo	3
Kobe	78	Toyota	565
Kochi	888	Yamagata	236
Kofu	552	Yokohama	45
Kumamoto	963	Yokosuka	468

Tours and Tour Guides

For English language tour information in Tokyo   592-1291
Japanese Association of Travel Agents (JATA)   270-5461

Train Ticket Prices

Current prices for Green Car and
Regular Class Service
are as follows:

Platform ticket (non-boarding only)   ¥1
Tokyo-Kyoto
  Green Car   ¥17,5
  Regular Reserved   ¥12,6
Tokyo-Osaka
  Green Car   ¥18,0
  Regular Reserved   ¥13,1
Tokyo-Hakata
  Green Car   ¥28,0
  Regular Reserved   ¥20,7

Bullet Train tickets cannot be purchased in the
United States, but some travel agencies can reserve
them when booking flights to Japan.

Railpass purchases are available only before arrival
in Japan. For information write Nippon Travel
Service in New York (212/986-7393).

Note: For transportation information to and
from airports, see Airports.

Translation And Interpretation Services

Tokyo

Simul International   586-8911
I.S.S. Inc.   230-4731
Japan Lingua   567-3814
Japan Convention Service   508-1215
Japan Guide Association   213-2706

Transportation Rates From Airport

Limousine Bus
(From Tokyo International Airport, Narita)

Airport to Tokyo (TCAT)	¥2,500
(90 minutes)	
Narita Airport to Haneda Airport	¥2,700
(100 minutes)	
To Yokohama City Air Terminal (YCAT)	¥3,100
(130 minutes)	

Taxi
(From Tokyo International Airport, Narita)

Airport to Downtown Tokyo	about ¥20,000
(60 to 70 minutes)	

Skyliner
(Keisei Line, Limited Express)

Narita Airport Station to Keisei Ueno Station	¥1,490
(60 minutes)	
Connecting bus from airport terminal to Narita Station	¥170
(6 minutes)	

J.R.
(Sobu Line)

Narita Airport Station to Tokyo Station	
Rapid (75 minutes)	¥1,060
Limited Express (65 minutes)	¥2,460
Connecting bus from airport terminal to	
J.R. Narita Station	¥370
(25 minutes)	

NOTES

NOTES